STAAR

Grade 8 Social Studies Assessment

SECRETS

Study Guide
Your Key to Exam Success

STAAR Test Review for the
State of Texas Assessments
of Academic Readiness

Dear Future Exam Success Story:

First of all, **THANK YOU** for purchasing Mometrix study materials!

Second, congratulations! You are one of the few determined test-takers who are committed to doing whatever it takes to excel on your exam. **You have come to the right place.** We developed these study materials with one goal in mind: to deliver you the information you need in a format that's concise and easy to use.

In addition to optimizing your guide for the content of the test, we've outlined our recommended steps for breaking down the preparation process into small, attainable goals so you can make sure you stay on track.

We've also analyzed the entire test-taking process, identifying the most common pitfalls and showing how you can overcome them and be ready for any curveball the test throws you.

Standardized testing is one of the biggest obstacles on your road to success, which only increases the importance of doing well in the high-pressure, high-stakes environment of test day. Your results on this test could have a significant impact on your future, and this guide provides the information and practical advice to help you achieve your full potential on test day.

Your success is our success

We would love to hear from you! If you would like to share the story of your exam success or if you have any questions or comments in regard to our products, please contact us at **800-673-8175** or **support@mometrix.com**.

Thanks again for your business and we wish you continued success!

Sincerely,
The Mometrix Test Preparation Team

Need more help? Check out our flashcards at: http://MometrixFlashcards.com/STAAR

TABLE OF CONTENTS

Introduction

Thank you for purchasing this resource! You have made the choice to prepare yourself for a test that could have a huge impact on your future, and this guide is designed to help you be fully ready for test day. Obviously, it's important to have a solid understanding of the test material, but you also need to be prepared for the unique environment and stressors of the test, so that you can perform to the best of your abilities.

For this purpose, the first section that appears in this guide is the **Secret Keys**. We've devoted countless hours to meticulously researching what works and what doesn't, and we've boiled down our findings to the five most impactful steps you can take to improve your performance on the test. We start at the beginning with study planning and move through the preparation process, all the way to the testing strategies that will help you get the most out of what you know when you're finally sitting in front of the test.

We recommend that you start preparing for your test as far in advance as possible. However, if you've bought this guide as a last-minute study resource and only have a few days before your test, we recommend that you skip over the first two Secret Keys since they address a long-term study plan.

If you struggle with **test anxiety**, we strongly encourage you to check out our recommendations for how you can overcome it. Test anxiety is a formidable foe, but it can be beaten, and we want to make sure you have the tools you need to defeat it.

Secret Key #1 – Plan Big, Study Small

There's a lot riding on your performance. If you want to ace this test, you're going to need to keep your skills sharp and the material fresh in your mind. You need a plan that lets you review everything you need to know while still fitting in your schedule. We'll break this strategy down into three categories.

Information Organization

Start with the information you already have: the official test outline. From this, you can make a complete list of all the concepts you need to cover before the test. Organize these concepts into groups that can be studied together, and create a list of any related vocabulary you need to learn so you can brush up on any difficult terms. You'll want to keep this vocabulary list handy once you actually start studying since you may need to add to it along the way.

Time Management

Once you have your set of study concepts, decide how to spread them out over the time you have left before the test. Break your study plan into small, clear goals so you have a manageable task for each day and know exactly what you're doing. Then just focus on one small step at a time. When you manage your time this way, you don't need to spend hours at a time studying. Studying a small block of content for a short period each day helps you retain information better and avoid stressing over how much you have left to do. You can relax knowing that you have a plan to cover everything in time. In order for this strategy to be effective though, you have to start studying early and stick to your schedule. Avoid the exhaustion and futility that comes from last-minute cramming!

Study Environment

The environment you study in has a big impact on your learning. Studying in a coffee shop, while probably more enjoyable, is not likely to be as fruitful as studying in a quiet room. It's important to keep distractions to a minimum. You're only planning to study for a short block of time, so make the most of it. Don't pause to check your phone or get up to find a snack. It's also important to **avoid multitasking**. Research has consistently shown that multitasking will make your studying dramatically less effective. Your study area should also be comfortable and well-lit so you don't have the distraction of straining your eyes or sitting on an uncomfortable chair.

The time of day you study is also important. You want to be rested and alert. Don't wait until just before bedtime. Study when you'll be most likely to comprehend and remember. Even better, if you know what time of day your test will be, set that time aside for study. That way your brain will be used to working on that subject at that specific time and you'll have a better chance of recalling information.

Finally, it can be helpful to team up with others who are studying for the same test. Your actual studying should be done in as isolated an environment as possible, but the work of organizing the information and setting up the study plan can be divided up. In between study sessions, you can discuss with your teammates the concepts that you're all studying and quiz each other on the details. Just be sure that your teammates are as serious about the test as you are. If you find that your study time is being replaced with social time, you might need to find a new team.

Secret Key #2 – Make Your Studying Count

You're devoting a lot of time and effort to preparing for this test, so you want to be absolutely certain it will pay off. This means doing more than just reading the content and hoping you can remember it on test day. It's important to make every minute of study count. There are two main areas you can focus on to make your studying count:

Retention

It doesn't matter how much time you study if you can't remember the material. You need to make sure you are retaining the concepts. To check your retention of the information you're learning, try recalling it at later times with minimal prompting. Try carrying around flashcards and glance at one or two from time to time or ask a friend who's also studying for the test to quiz you.

To enhance your retention, look for ways to put the information into practice so that you can apply it rather than simply recalling it. If you're using the information in practical ways, it will be much easier to remember. Similarly, it helps to solidify a concept in your mind if you're not only reading it to yourself but also explaining it to someone else. Ask a friend to let you teach them about a concept you're a little shaky on (or speak aloud to an imaginary audience if necessary). As you try to summarize, define, give examples, and answer your friend's questions, you'll understand the concepts better and they will stay with you longer. Finally, step back for a big picture view and ask yourself how each piece of information fits with the whole subject. When you link the different concepts together and see them working together as a whole, it's easier to remember the individual components.

Finally, practice showing your work on any multi-step problems, even if you're just studying. Writing out each step you take to solve a problem will help solidify the process in your mind, and you'll be more likely to remember it during the test.

Modality

Modality simply refers to the means or method by which you study. Choosing a study modality that fits your own individual learning style is crucial. No two people learn best in exactly the same way, so it's important to know your strengths and use them to your advantage.

For example, if you learn best by visualization, focus on visualizing a concept in your mind and draw an image or a diagram. Try color-coding your notes, illustrating them, or creating symbols that will trigger your mind to recall a learned concept. If you learn best by hearing or discussing information, find a study partner who learns the same way or read aloud to yourself. Think about how to put the information in your own words. Imagine that you are giving a lecture on the topic and record yourself so you can listen to it later.

For any learning style, flashcards can be helpful. Organize the information so you can take advantage of spare moments to review. Underline key words or phrases. Use different colors for different categories. Mnemonic devices (such as creating a short list in which every item starts with the same letter) can also help with retention. Find what works best for you and use it to store the information in your mind most effectively and easily.

Secret Key #3 – Practice the Right Way

Your success on test day depends not only on how many hours you put into preparing, but also on whether you prepared the right way. It's good to check along the way to see if your studying is paying off. One of the most effective ways to do this is by taking practice tests to evaluate your progress. Practice tests are useful because they show exactly where you need to improve. Every time you take a practice test, pay special attention to these three groups of questions:

- The questions you got wrong
- The questions you had to guess on, even if you guessed right
- The questions you found difficult or slow to work through

This will show you exactly what your weak areas are, and where you need to devote more study time. Ask yourself why each of these questions gave you trouble. Was it because you didn't understand the material? Was it because you didn't remember the vocabulary? Do you need more repetitions on this type of question to build speed and confidence? Dig into those questions and figure out how you can strengthen your weak areas as you go back to review the material.

Additionally, many practice tests have a section explaining the answer choices. It can be tempting to read the explanation and think that you now have a good understanding of the concept. However, an explanation likely only covers part of the question's broader context. Even if the explanation makes sense, **go back and investigate** every concept related to the question until you're positive you have a thorough understanding.

As you go along, keep in mind that the practice test is just that: practice. Memorizing these questions and answers will not be very helpful on the actual test because it is unlikely to have any of the same exact questions. If you only know the right answers to the sample questions, you won't be prepared for the real thing. **Study the concepts** until you understand them fully, and then you'll be able to answer any question that shows up on the test.

It's important to wait on the practice tests until you're ready. If you take a test on your first day of study, you may be overwhelmed by the amount of material covered and how much you need to learn. Work up to it gradually.

On test day, you'll need to be prepared for answering questions, managing your time, and using the test-taking strategies you've learned. It's a lot to balance, like a mental marathon that will have a big impact on your future. Like training for a marathon, you'll need to start slowly and work your way up. When test day arrives, you'll be ready.

Start with the strategies you've read in the first two Secret Keys—plan your course and study in the way that works best for you. If you have time, consider using multiple study resources to get different approaches to the same concepts. It can be helpful to see difficult concepts from more than one angle. Then find a good source for practice tests. Many times, the test website will suggest potential study resources or provide sample tests.

Practice Test Strategy

When you're ready to start taking practice tests, follow this strategy:

Untimed and Open-Book Practice

Take the first test with no time constraints and with your notes and study guide handy. Take your time and focus on applying the strategies you've learned.

Timed and Open-Book Practice

Take the second practice test open-book as well, but set a timer and practice pacing yourself to finish in time.

Timed and Closed-Book Practice

Take any other practice tests as if it were test day. Set a timer and put away your study materials. Sit at a table or desk in a quiet room, imagine yourself at the testing center, and answer questions as quickly and accurately as possible.

Keep repeating timed and closed-book tests on a regular basis until you run out of practice tests or it's time for the actual test. Your mind will be ready for the schedule and stress of test day, and you'll be able to focus on recalling the material you've learned.

Secret Key #4 – Pace Yourself

Once you're fully prepared for the material on the test, your biggest challenge on test day will be managing your time. Just knowing that the clock is ticking can make you panic even if you have plenty of time left. Work on pacing yourself so you can build confidence against the time constraints of the exam. Pacing is a difficult skill to master, especially in a high-pressure environment, so **practice is vital**.

Set time expectations for your pace based on how much time is available. For example, if a section has 60 questions and the time limit is 30 minutes, you know you have to average 30 seconds or less per question in order to answer them all. Although 30 seconds is the hard limit, set 25 seconds per question as your goal, so you reserve extra time to spend on harder questions. When you budget extra time for the harder questions, you no longer have any reason to stress when those questions take longer to answer.

Don't let this time expectation distract you from working through the test at a calm, steady pace, but keep it in mind so you don't spend too much time on any one question. Recognize that taking extra time on one question you don't understand may keep you from answering two that you do understand later in the test. If your time limit for a question is up and you're still not sure of the answer, mark it and move on, and come back to it later if the time and the test format allow. If the testing format doesn't allow you to return to earlier questions, just make an educated guess; then put it out of your mind and move on.

On the easier questions, be careful not to rush. It may seem wise to hurry through them so you have more time for the challenging ones, but it's not worth missing one if you know the concept and just didn't take the time to read the question fully. Work efficiently but make sure you understand the question and have looked at all of the answer choices, since more than one may seem right at first.

Even if you're paying attention to the time, you may find yourself a little behind at some point. You should speed up to get back on track, but do so wisely. Don't panic; just take a few seconds less on each question until you're caught up. Don't guess without thinking, but do look through the answer choices and eliminate any you know are wrong. If you can get down to two choices, it is often worthwhile to guess from those. Once you've chosen an answer, move on and don't dwell on any that you skipped or had to hurry through. If a question was taking too long, chances are it was one of the harder ones, so you weren't as likely to get it right anyway.

On the other hand, if you find yourself getting ahead of schedule, it may be beneficial to slow down a little. The more quickly you work, the more likely you are to make a careless mistake that will affect your score. You've budgeted time for each question, so don't be afraid to spend that time. Practice an efficient but careful pace to get the most out of the time you have.

Secret Key #5 – Have a Plan for Guessing

When you're taking the test, you may find yourself stuck on a question. Some of the answer choices seem better than others, but you don't see the one answer choice that is obviously correct. What do you do?

The scenario described above is very common, yet most test takers have not effectively prepared for it. Developing and practicing a plan for guessing may be one of the single most effective uses of your time as you get ready for the exam.

In developing your plan for guessing, there are three questions to address:

- When should you start the guessing process?
- How should you narrow down the choices?
- Which answer should you choose?

When to Start the Guessing Process

Unless your plan for guessing is to select C every time (which, despite its merits, is not what we recommend), you need to leave yourself enough time to apply your answer elimination strategies. Since you have a limited amount of time for each question, that means that if you're going to give yourself the best shot at guessing correctly, you have to decide quickly whether or not you will guess.

Of course, the best-case scenario is that you don't have to guess at all, so first, see if you can answer the question based on your knowledge of the subject and basic reasoning skills. Focus on the key words in the question and try to jog your memory of related topics. Give yourself a chance to bring the knowledge to mind, but once you realize that you don't have (or you can't access) the knowledge you need to answer the question, it's time to start the guessing process.

It's almost always better to start the guessing process too early than too late. It only takes a few seconds to remember something and answer the question from knowledge. Carefully eliminating wrong answer choices takes longer. Plus, going through the process of eliminating answer choices can actually help jog your memory.

Summary: Start the guessing process as soon as you decide that you can't answer the question based on your knowledge.

How to Narrow Down the Choices

The next chapter in this book (**Test-Taking Strategies**) includes a wide range of strategies for how to approach questions and how to look for answer choices to eliminate. You will definitely want to read those carefully, practice them, and figure out which ones work best for you. Here though, we're going to address a mindset rather than a particular strategy.

Your chances of guessing an answer correctly depend on how many options you are choosing from.

How many choices you have	How likely you are to guess correctly
5	20%
4	25%
3	33%
2	50%
1	100%

You can see from this chart just how valuable it is to be able to eliminate incorrect answers and make an educated guess, but there are two things that many test takers do that cause them to miss out on the benefits of guessing:

- Accidentally eliminating the correct answer
- Selecting an answer based on an impression

We'll look at the first one here, and the second one in the next section.

To avoid accidentally eliminating the correct answer, we recommend a thought exercise called **the $5 challenge**. In this challenge, you only eliminate an answer choice from contention if you are willing to bet $5 on it being wrong. Why $5? Five dollars is a small but not insignificant amount of money. It's an amount you could afford to lose but wouldn't want to throw away. And while losing $5 once might not hurt too much, doing it twenty times will set you back $100. In the same way, each small decision you make—eliminating a choice here, guessing on a question there—won't by itself impact your score very much, but when you put them all together, they can make a big difference. By holding each answer choice elimination decision to a higher standard, you can reduce the risk of accidentally eliminating the correct answer.

The $5 challenge can also be applied in a positive sense: If you are willing to bet $5 that an answer choice *is* correct, go ahead and mark it as correct.

Summary: Only eliminate an answer choice if you are willing to bet $5 that it is wrong.

Which Answer to Choose

You're taking the test. You've run into a hard question and decided you'll have to guess. You've eliminated all the answer choices you're willing to bet $5 on. Now you have to pick an answer. Why do we even need to talk about this? Why can't you just pick whichever one you feel like when the time comes?

The answer to these questions is that if you don't come into the test with a plan, you'll rely on your impression to select an answer choice, and if you do that, you risk falling into a trap. The test writers know that everyone who takes their test will be guessing on some of the questions, so they intentionally write wrong answer choices to seem plausible. You still have to pick an answer though, and if the wrong answer choices are designed to look right, how can you ever be sure that you're not falling for their trap? The best solution we've found to this dilemma is to take the decision out of your hands entirely. Here is the process we recommend:

Once you've eliminated any choices that you are confident (willing to bet $5) are wrong, select the first remaining choice as your answer.

Whether you choose to select the first remaining choice, the second, or the last, the important thing is that you use some preselected standard. Using this approach guarantees that you will not be enticed into selecting an answer choice that looks right, because you are not basing your decision on how the answer choices look.

This is not meant to make you question your knowledge. Instead, it is to help you recognize the difference between your knowledge and your impressions. There's a huge difference between thinking an answer is right because of what you know, and thinking an answer is right because it looks or sounds like it should be right.

Summary: To ensure that your selection is appropriately random, make a predetermined selection from among all answer choices you have not eliminated.

Test-Taking Strategies

This section contains a list of test-taking strategies that you may find helpful as you work through the test. By taking what you know and applying logical thought, you can maximize your chances of answering any question correctly!

It is very important to realize that every question is different and every person is different: no single strategy will work on every question, and no single strategy will work for every person. That's why we've included all of them here, so you can try them out and determine which ones work best for different types of questions and which ones work best for you.

Question Strategies

Read Carefully

Read the question and answer choices carefully. Don't miss the question because you misread the terms. You have plenty of time to read each question thoroughly and make sure you understand what is being asked. Yet a happy medium must be attained, so don't waste too much time. You must read carefully, but efficiently.

Contextual Clues

Look for contextual clues. If the question includes a word you are not familiar with, look at the immediate context for some indication of what the word might mean. Contextual clues can often give you all the information you need to decipher the meaning of an unfamiliar word. Even if you can't determine the meaning, you may be able to narrow down the possibilities enough to make a solid guess at the answer to the question.

Prefixes

If you're having trouble with a word in the question or answer choices, try dissecting it. Take advantage of every clue that the word might include. Prefixes and suffixes can be a huge help. Usually they allow you to determine a basic meaning. Pre- means before, post- means after, pro - is positive, de- is negative. From prefixes and suffixes, you can get an idea of the general meaning of the word and try to put it into context.

Hedge Words

Watch out for critical hedge words, such as *likely, may, can, sometimes, often, almost, mostly, usually, generally, rarely,* and *sometimes.* Question writers insert these hedge phrases to cover every possibility. Often an answer choice will be wrong simply because it leaves no room for exception. Be on guard for answer choices that have definitive words such as *exactly* and *always.*

Switchback Words

Stay alert for *switchbacks.* These are the words and phrases frequently used to alert you to shifts in thought. The most common switchback words are *but, although,* and *however.* Others include *nevertheless, on the other hand, even though, while, in spite of, despite, regardless of.* Switchback words are important to catch because they can change the direction of the question or an answer choice.

Face Value

When in doubt, use common sense. Accept the situation in the problem at face value. Don't read too much into it. These problems will not require you to make wild assumptions. If you have to go beyond creativity and warp time or space in order to have an answer choice fit the question, then you should move on and consider the other answer choices. These are normal problems rooted in reality. The applicable relationship or explanation may not be readily apparent, but it is there for you to figure out. Use your common sense to interpret anything that isn't clear.

Answer Choice Strategies

Answer Selection

The most thorough way to pick an answer choice is to identify and eliminate wrong answers until only one is left, then confirm it is the correct answer. Sometimes an answer choice may immediately seem right, but be careful. The test writers will usually put more than one reasonable answer choice on each question, so take a second to read all of them and make sure that the other choices are not equally obvious. As long as you have time left, it is better to read every answer choice than to pick the first one that looks right without checking the others.

Answer Choice Families

An answer choice family consists of two (in rare cases, three) answer choices that are very similar in construction and cannot all be true at the same time. If you see two answer choices that are direct opposites or parallels, one of them is usually the correct answer. For instance, if one answer choice says that quantity x increases and another either says that quantity x decreases (opposite) or says that quantity y increases (parallel), then those answer choices would fall into the same family. An answer choice that doesn't match the construction of the answer choice family is more likely to be incorrect. Most questions will not have answer choice families, but when they do appear, you should be prepared to recognize them.

Eliminate Answers

Eliminate answer choices as soon as you realize they are wrong, but make sure you consider all possibilities. If you are eliminating answer choices and realize that the last one you are left with is also wrong, don't panic. Start over and consider each choice again. There may be something you missed the first time that you will realize on the second pass.

Avoid Fact Traps

Don't be distracted by an answer choice that is factually true but doesn't answer the question. You are looking for the choice that answers the question. Stay focused on what the question is asking for so you don't accidentally pick an answer that is true but incorrect. Always go back to the question and make sure the answer choice you've selected actually answers the question and is not merely a true statement.

Extreme Statements

In general, you should avoid answers that put forth extreme actions as standard practice or proclaim controversial ideas as established fact. An answer choice that states the "process should be used in certain situations, if..." is much more likely to be correct than one that states the "process should be discontinued completely." The first is a calm rational statement and doesn't even make a definitive, uncompromising stance, using a hedge word *if* to provide wiggle room, whereas the second choice is a radical idea and far more extreme.

Benchmark

As you read through the answer choices and you come across one that seems to answer the question well, mentally select that answer choice. This is not your final answer, but it's the one that will help you evaluate the other answer choices. The one that you selected is your benchmark or standard for judging each of the other answer choices. Every other answer choice must be compared to your benchmark. That choice is correct until proven otherwise by another answer choice beating it. If you find a better answer, then that one becomes your new benchmark. Once you've decided that no other choice answers the question as well as your benchmark, you have your final answer.

Predict the Answer

Before you even start looking at the answer choices, it is often best to try to predict the answer. When you come up with the answer on your own, it is easier to avoid distractions and traps because you will know exactly what to look for. The right answer choice is unlikely to be word-for-word what you came up with, but it should be a close match. Even if you are confident that you have the right answer, you should still take the time to read each option before moving on.

General Strategies

Tough Questions

If you are stumped on a problem or it appears too hard or too difficult, don't waste time. Move on! Remember though, if you can quickly check for obviously incorrect answer choices, your chances of guessing correctly are greatly improved. Before you completely give up, at least try to knock out a couple of possible answers. Eliminate what you can and then guess at the remaining answer choices before moving on.

Check Your Work

Since you will probably not know every term listed and the answer to every question, it is important that you get credit for the ones that you do know. Don't miss any questions through careless mistakes. If at all possible, try to take a second to look back over your answer selection and make sure you've selected the correct answer choice and haven't made a costly careless mistake (such as marking an answer choice that you didn't mean to mark). This quick double check should more than pay for itself in caught mistakes for the time it costs.

Pace Yourself

It's easy to be overwhelmed when you're looking at a page full of questions; your mind is confused and full of random thoughts, and the clock is ticking down faster than you would like. Calm down and maintain the pace that you have set for yourself. Especially as you get down to the last few minutes of the test, don't let the small numbers on the clock make you panic. As long as you are on track by monitoring your pace, you are guaranteed to have time for each question.

Don't Rush

It is very easy to make errors when you are in a hurry. Maintaining a fast pace in answering questions is pointless if it makes you miss questions that you would have gotten right otherwise. Test writers like to include distracting information and wrong answers that seem right. Taking a little extra time to avoid careless mistakes can make all the difference in your test score. Find a pace that allows you to be confident in the answers that you select.

Keep Moving

Panicking will not help you pass the test, so do your best to stay calm and keep moving. Taking deep breaths and going through the answer elimination steps you practiced can help to break through a stress barrier and keep your pace.

Final Notes

The combination of a solid foundation of content knowledge and the confidence that comes from practicing your plan for applying that knowledge is the key to maximizing your performance on test day. As your foundation of content knowledge is built up and strengthened, you'll find that the strategies included in this chapter become more and more effective in helping you quickly sift through the distractions and traps of the test to isolate the correct answer.

Now it's time to move on to the test content chapters of this book, but be sure to keep your goal in mind. As you read, think about how you will be able to apply this information on the test. If you've already seen sample questions for the test and you have an idea of the question format and style, try to come up with questions of your own that you can answer based on what you're reading. This will give you valuable practice applying your knowledge in the same ways you can expect to on test day.

Good luck and good studying!

Social Studies Assessment

History

Jamestown

The first permanent English settlement, Jamestown, was established in North America in 1607. The Virginia Company of London started the colony and named it after King James I of England. Several factors contributed to the establishment of the colony. England and Spain were experiencing a period of peace. The Virginia Company provided financial support for colonization and was able to find willing settlers. Those settlers were lured by the prospects of adventure and religious freedom. In addition, they were able to continue being English subjects.

Original 13 colonies

Reasons for the establishment

The original 13 colonies were started by settlers from England. These people came to the New World for many reasons, including political ideology, economic prospects, and social change. People who disagreed with Britain's policies may have wanted to start a new society. Companies wanted to own land in the Americas as a way to increase profits. Settlers who came for economic reasons thought they could make money on goods not found in Europe, like tobacco. Many others came for social reasons, the most important of which was religious freedom.

Representative government

A representative government allows the people to choose who will represent them in governmental decisions. Each colony was given the opportunity to choose representatives, an action that is the mainstay of American democracy to this day. The colonists did not like the tariffs imposed upon them by King George III and did not want a system without checks and balances to occur in the colonies. A representative government allowed the colonists to keep the interests of the people in mind, rather than impose laws produced by a monarchy. Citizens could vote on candidates that would vote for them on the local, state, and federal level, since most citizens had other jobs to attend to. Representatives could be voted out of office if they did not represent the interests of the people. This allowed colonists to have a means of control over tariffs and laws that affected their own lives.

Benjamin Franklin

Benjamin Franklin was one of the Founding Fathers of the United States of America. Among many other things, Franklin was in favor of colonial unity and thought the colonies should band together to create an independent nation. During the American Revolution, Franklin was a diplomat who went to Europe and worked to secure France's support for the colonists seeking independence from Britain. Without the support of France, the colonists would not have successfully gained independence. Franklin's work was instrumental in the development of the United States of America. Only a month after his return from France, Benjamin Franklin helped draft the Declaration of Independence.

Thomas Paine, King George III, and the Marquis de Lafayette

The contributions of Thomas Paine, King George III, and the Marquis de Lafayette to the American Revolution are as follows:

- Thomas Paine, often described as the Father of the American Revolution, wrote *Common Sense*, a pro-independence pamphlet published in 1776. It used a new style of political writing to promote the American Revolution and democratic government and denounce British tyranny. *Common Sense* became very popular, serving as a rallying point for American revolutionaries.
- King George III was the king of Great Britain during the American Revolution, and was responsible for waging war against the colonies. He was criticized heavily in the Declaration of Independence.
- The Marquis de Lafayette was a French military general who served during the American Revolution under the command of George Washington. He played an important role in the siege at Yorktown, where he contained British forces long enough for reinforcements to arrive. The British were defeated, which ended the war.

Virginia House of Burgesses

The Virginia House of Burgesses was the first elected legislative body in North America. The word *burgess* refers to a municipal official or a representative of a borough, as it was used in the English House of Commons. The House of Burgesses was established by the Virginia Company, the same private company that founded the Virginia Colony, under a royal charter. On July 30, 1619, the House held its first legislative assembly, but it only lasted six days due to an outbreak of malaria.

Mayflower Compact

The Mayflower Compact of 1620 was the governing document of Plymouth Colony. The Pilgrims who came to North America aboard the *Mayflower* created the document to help organize their community. All 41 of the adult males signed the contract. The settlers knew that previous colonies had failed due to lack of government. The major idea of the compact was that the colony was to be free of English rule and that the colonists would create their own government. The Mayflower Compact was important because it was the first document to establish a community on North America that did not feel allegiance to the King of England. The central idea of self-rule paved the way for the American Revolution.

Fundamental Orders of Connecticut

The Fundamental Orders of Connecticut documented the structure of the government of the Connecticut Colony. They were adopted by the Connecticut Colony council in 1639. They are considered by many historians to be the first written constitution of a Western civilization. This is why Connecticut holds the state nickname of *The Constitution State*. The Orders are a short document, but contain several of the same principles that were later used in drafting the US Constitution. The Orders state the powers of the government as well as the rights of the individual, and how those rights are ensured by the government.

Causes of the American Revolution

Colonists became increasingly frustrated with Britain's policies. After the French and Indian War, Britain badly needed money. King George III was seeking to increase revenues, and this usually meant more taxes for the colonists. In addition, the Proclamation of 1763 forbade colonists from settling west of the Appalachian Mountains. Many colonists thought this unfairly limited their economic pursuits. Tensions regarding land and taxation continued to grow at a time when John Locke's ideas on natural rights and the social contract became popular. Locke argued that people allow the government to govern them and if the government becomes tyrannical and takes away natural rights, the people have the right to rebel. All of these were factors in the colonists revolting against the British government.

Stamp Act

The Stamp Act of 1765 was levied without the consent of the colonists. It specified that a stamp must be applied to all legal documents (there was considerable debate over the definition of this phrase) indicating that a tax had been paid for the defense of the colonies. This act was extremely unpopular, perhaps most because its presence was so visible; its implementation generated loud cries of "taxation without representation." The British responded by claiming that the colonists had "virtual representation" by members of Parliament. The colonists continued to claim that they needed direct and actual representation, although many feared that even if they were to get it, they would probably lose most votes anyway.

Battles of the Revolutionary War

The Battle of Lexington and Concord (April, 1775) is considered the first engagement of the Revolutionary War. The Battle of Bunker Hill, in June of 1775, was one of the bloodiest of the entire war. Although American troops withdrew, about half the British army was lost. The colonists proved they could stand against professional British soldiers. In August, Britain declared that the American colonies were officially in a state of rebellion. The first colonial victory occurred in Trenton, New Jersey, when Washington and his troops crossed the Delaware River on Christmas Day, 1776 for a December 26, surprise attack on British and Hessian troops. The Battle of Saratoga effectively ended a plan to separate the New England colonies from their Southern counterparts. The surrender of British general John Burgoyne led to France joining the war as allies of the Americans, and is generally considered a turning point of the war. On October 19, 1781, General Cornwallis surrendered after a defeat in the Battle of Yorktown, Virginia, ending the Revolutionary War.

Declaration of Independence

The 13 colonies asserted their independence from England in 1776 with the adoption of the Declaration of Independence. In June 1776, Congress appointed a committee to draft a document to explain to the world why the colonies wanted independence. The goal was to gain international support. The document that was created was the Declaration of Independence, which argued for the "unalienable rights" of all people, among other things. On July 4, 1776, the Declaration of Independence was approved by all of the representatives from all 13 colonies.

Samuel Adams

Samuel Adams was one of the leaders of the American Revolution, and one of the key minds behind the political philosophies that shaped the United States government. He graduated from Harvard College but was an unsuccessful businessman before he began concentrating on a career in politics. He held various positions in colonial Massachusetts and later in the Massachusetts state government including Governor, Lieutenant Governor, and President of the Senate. As an influential political figure, he was instrumental in convincing the Continental Congress to issue the Declaration of Independence. He was also adept at swaying public opinion, using his influence to stir up anger against the British for their violations of the colonists' liberty.

Wentworth Cheswell

Wentworth Cheswell was an African-American teacher and veteran of the Revolutionary War, who served in several positions in the local government of Newmarket, New Hampshire. Despite being only one-quarter African and being listed in the census as white, Cheswell is commonly regarded as the first African-American to be elected to a public office in the state of New Hampshire. In 1768, he was elected to his first public office as a constable. This began a stretch of nearly 50 years of public service, ending with his death in 1817. Cheswell was elected to public office almost every year for the rest of his life.

Articles of Confederation

The Articles of Confederation were the first Constitution of the United States. When fully ratified in 1781, it established a union of the states. Some of the strengths of the Articles of Confederation are that it created a union in which states could act together to declare war and negotiate agreements. The major weakness of the document was that the federal government could not collect taxes. Each state had to agree to give the federal government funds. In addition, the document did not create a fair balance between the large and small states in terms of legislative decision-making and funding. Each state was given one vote, but large states were expected to contribute more money.

Treaty of Paris

The Treaty of Paris was signed on September 3, 1783, bringing an official end to the Revolutionary War. In this document, Britain officially recognized the United States of America as an independent nation. The treaty established the Mississippi River as the country's western border. The treaty also restored Florida to Spain, while France reclaimed African and Caribbean colonies seized by the British in 1763. On November 24, 1783, the last British troops departed from the newly born United States of America.

Philadelphia Convention of 1787

The Philadelphia Convention is also known as the Constitutional Convention. Arguments for and against ratification of the constitution were presented at the convention by the Federalists and anti-Federalists, respectively. The Federalists supported ratification because they felt that the Constitution would allow the people to protect their freedom and rights. The anti-Federalists argued that the Constitution was too centralizing—that is, put too much power in the hands of the federal government--and would destroy the liberty so hard won in the American Revolution. The Federalists were very well organized and had strong political support. The anti-Federalists were a much more loosely formed group. A lively newspaper debate occurred before each state voted on ratification.

Northwest Ordinance

The Northwest Ordinance is considered one of the most important aspects of the Articles of Confederation and has had a lasting impact. Passed in 1787, the Northwest Ordinance made provisions for setting up governments in the western territories. With such governments, these territories eventually could join the Union and be equal with the original 13 states. The Northwest Ordinance is the reason that the United States was able to grow. Because of the ordinance, the United States expanded westward by the creation of new states instead of expanding the existing ones. The Northwest Territories referenced in the document included parts of Illinois, Ohio, Indiana, Michigan, Wisconsin, and parts of Minnesota. According to the ordinance, after 5,000 adult males moved into a territory, they could form a general assembly and send a nonvoting delegate to

Congress. When 60,000 people moved into a territory, they could draft and submit a constitution. If approved, the territory could become a state. The first state created from a territory was Ohio, in 1803.

John Adams

John Adams became the second president of the United States in the election of 1796; his opponent, Thomas Jefferson, became vice president because he received the second-most electoral votes. Adams was immediately confronted by the French, who were angry about the Jay Treaty and the broken Treaty of Alliance of 1788. After the French began destroying American ships, Adams sent American diplomats to meet with the French ambassador Talleyrand, who demanded tribute and then snubbed the Americans. There followed an undeclared naval war between 1798 and 1800. During which, the American military grew rapidly, warships were built and the Department of the Navy was established. Finally, at the Convention of 1800, the Treaty of Alliance of 1778 was torn up and it was agreed in this new Treaty of Mortefontaine that the Americans would pay for damages done to their ships by the French, among a host of other clauses including each country giving the other Most Favored Nation trade status.

Abigail Adams

Abigail Adams, wife of John Adams, was the second First Lady of the United States and the mother of John Quincy Adams, the sixth President. Her life is one of the most well-documented of any of the early first ladies, due mainly to her extensively preserved written correspondence with her husband, who frequently sought her advice on all manner of topics related to government and politics. Adams was a prominent advocate of women's rights. She believed that women deserved more opportunities, particularly with regard to education and bettering themselves intellectually.

Mercy Otis Warren

Mercy Otis Warren was a female political writer during the time of the American Revolution. She wrote on topics such as politics and war, which at the time were considered to be the domain of men. She had no formal education, but was nonetheless a great thinker and writer. At the time, there were few people who were qualified to address subjects such as these, which allowed her a niche. She did most of her political writing under the pseudonym "A Columbian Patriot," but in 1790, she published a collection of poems and plays under her real name. In 1805, she published the first history of the Revolution authored by a woman, a three-volume book titled *History of the Rise, Progress, and Termination of the American Revolution*.

Development of political parties

George Washington was adamantly against the establishment of political parties, based on the abuses perpetrated by such parties in Britain. However, political parties developed in US politics almost from the beginning. Major parties throughout US History have included:

- Federalists and Democratic-Republicans—formed in the late 1700s and disagreed on the balance of power between national and state government.
- Democrats and Whigs—developed before the Civil War, based on disagreements about various issues such as slavery.
- Democrats and Republicans—developed after the Civil War, with issues centering on the treatment of the post-war South.
- While third parties sometimes enter the picture in US politics, the government is basically a two-party system, dominated by the Democrats and Republicans.

Washington's accomplishments and Farewell Address

In 1796, Washington decided he was too tired to continue as president. In his famous Farewell Address, he implored the United States to avoid three things: permanent alliances; political factions; and sectionalism. Washington felt that the nation could only be successful if people placed the nation ahead of their own region. For his own part, Washington made some significant improvements during his presidency. He avoided war at a time when the nation was vulnerable. He also avoided political alliances and promoted the national government without alienating great numbers of people. Washington oversaw Hamilton's creation of the economic system and guided expansion to the West (as well as the creation of three new states: Vermont, Kentucky, and Tennessee).

Louisiana Purchase

In 1803 the United States acquired the Louisiana Territory from France. The U.S. government, which was led by President Thomas Jefferson, purchased the territory from Napoleon Bonaparte, ruler of France, for $15 million. The land area of the United States more than doubled with the purchase, which included all of the land from the Mississippi River to the Rocky Mountains. This land was full of fertile plains and vital waterways, and later became all or part of 13 states: Louisiana, Missouri, Arkansas, Iowa, Minnesota, Kansas, Nebraska, Colorado, North Dakota, South Dakota, Montana, Wyoming, and Oklahoma.

Physical characteristics compared to original 13 colonies

The original 13 states were located along the East Coast of North America. The land was close to water. Proximity to water is vital to settlement for many reasons. Goods can be brought in and sent out, and water is needed to successfully grow crops. Almost all of the land gained from the Louisiana Purchase was inland. Only the southern tip of Louisiana is located on water. Most of the land is flat prairie, much of it good farmland. After the acquisition of this land, surveyors were sent to bring back information about the quality of the land to those living in the East who were interested in moving West.

War of 1812

The War of 1812 grew out of the continuing tension between France and Great Britain. Napoleon continued to strive to conquer Britain, while the U.S. continued trade with both countries, but favoring France and the French colonies. Because of what Britain saw as an alliance between America and France, they determined to bring an end to trade between the two nations. With the British preventing U.S. trade with the French and the French preventing trade with the British, James Madison's presidency introduced acts to regulate international trade. If either Britain or France removed their restrictions, America would not trade with the other. Napoleon acted first, and Madison prohibited trade with England. England saw this as the U.S. formally siding with the French, and war ensued in 1812. The War of 1812 has been called the Second American Revolution. It established the superiority of the U.S. naval forces and reestablished U.S. independence from Britain and Europe.

The War of 1812 did not really accomplish its supposed goal of establishing neutral trading rights for American ships. The exodus of Napoleon during the war made this a moot point. Nevertheless, from Madison's perspective the war could only be seen as a major success. The United States lost no major territory, and scored enough victories to keep the British from making any extreme demands. More importantly, perhaps, Americans were overjoyed that the US was finally getting respect from the major European powers. Nationalism exploded in the US: people forgot the debacle of the failed national bank, and the economy boomed. Finally, the success of the War of 1812 effectively drove the final nail into the coffin of the Federalist party.

John Quincy Adams

All the major candidates in the 1824 election were Democrat-Republicans. Although Andrew Jackson received more electoral votes than John Quincy Adams, he did not win a majority, and Adams (with the help of Henry Clay) won the run-off in the House of Representatives. Adams was a fierce nationalist at a time when many in the country were sectionalist. Although his initiatives for a national university and public funding for the arts were well-meaning, Adams was still believed to be out of touch with the common man. He further alienated the middle and lower classes with the Tariff of 1828, known in the South as the "Tariff of Abominations." The South was already on shaky economic ground and the tariff became a scapegoat for its troubles. John C. Calhoun was an especially ardent Southern voice; he futilely proposed that states should have the ability to nullify federal regulations.

Monroe Doctrine

The Monroe Doctrine was a statement of foreign policy created by President James Monroe and Secretary of State John Quincy Adams. The document stated that Europe should not interfere in affairs within the United States or with the creation of other countries in the Western Hemisphere. Likewise, the United States would not get involved in European matters. In 1823, when the doctrine was announced, the United States was facing Russian claims to the Northwest Coast, and governments in Latin America wanted independence from Spain. The doctrine reflected growing nationalism and a decreased interest in international affairs. President Polk revived the doctrine in 1845, and it continued to be important ideologically into the next century.

Andrew Jackson

Andrew Jackson is often seen as a symbol of the rising power of the New West, or as an embodiment of the "rags to riches" fable. He spent much of his presidency trying to promote the idea of nationalism at a time when most of the country was ardently sectionalist. During his presidency, he dominated Congress, vetoing more legislation than all of the previous presidents combined. He was also famous for his so-called "Kitchen Cabinet," a group of close advisers without official positions. Many of these men later received formal appointments, including as Secretary of State (Martin van Buren), Postmaster General (Amos Kendall), and Secretary of the Treasury (Roger B. Taney). The election of 1828 is considered the first modern campaign in American politics. Andrew Jackson had the first campaign manager, Amos Kendall, and produced buttons, posters, and slogans to support his candidacy. These men—Jackson, Kendall, John C. Calhoun, and Martin van Buren—formed the beginning of the Democratic party. Meanwhile, the incumbent John Quincy Adams ran a very formal campaign, with little of the "flesh-pressing" of Jackson. Adams tried to discredit Jackson as an adulterer and bigamist because Jackson's wife had not been officially divorced at the time of their marriage. When his wife died during the campaign, however, the popular sentiment returned to Jackson, and he won the election by a considerable margin. Jackson's inauguration was an over-crowded, chaotic affair; the president suffered three cracked ribs during the festivities.

Second Great Awakening

Led by Protestant evangelical leaders, the Second Great Awakening occurred between 1800 and 1830. Several missionary groups grew out of the movement, including the American Home Missionary Society, which formed in 1826. The ideas behind the Second Great Awakening focused on personal responsibility, both as an individual and in response to injustice and suffering. The American Bible Society and the American Tract Society provided literature, while various traveling preachers spread the word. New denominations arose, including the Latter Day Saints and Seventh-Day Adventists.

Another movement associated with the Second Great Awakening was the temperance movement, focused on ending the production and use of alcohol. One major organization behind the temperance movement was the Society for the Promotion of Temperance, formed in 1826 in Boston, Massachusetts.

Manifest Destiny

Manifest Destiny was the popular belief in the 1840s that the United States was destined to cover the entire area from the Atlantic Ocean to the Pacific Ocean. Manifest Destiny led to the acquisition of the Oregon Territory from Britain during the presidency of James Polk in the 1840s. After the Mexican War of 1848, a large swath of southwest territory was gained as well. This included the land of California, Nevada, and Utah, and parts of Arizona, Colorado, New Mexico, and Wyoming.

U.S.-Mexican War

The immediate causes of the Mexican War were the American annexation of Texas, disputes over the Southern border of Texas and the large amount of money owed to the United States by Mexico. Moreover, it was well known that the Mexicans held the US in contempt, considering them greedy land-grabbers. Polk sent an emissary to buy Texas, California, and some Mexican territory for $30 million; he was refused. Zachary Taylor then led an American expedition into a disputed area of Texas where some of them were killed. Polk was able to use these deaths as a rationale for war, despite considerable opposition in Congress. Overall, the Democrats supported the war, while the Whigs, led in part by Abraham Lincoln, were opposed.

Abraham Lincoln

Abraham Lincoln, the 16th President of the United States, is best known for leading the country through the Civil War. Lincoln began his political career in 1832 at the age 23 when he ran for the Illinois General Assembly. He lost that election but on his second attempt two years later, he was elected. In 1846, Lincoln was elected to a single term in the U.S. House of Representatives. After serving his two-year term, he returned to Springfield to practice law. In the presidential race of 1860, Lincoln defeated Stephen Douglas, John Breckinridge, and John Bell to become the 16th President of the United States. By February of 1861, seven states had seceded from the Union and formed the Confederate States of America.

On April 12, 1861, Confederate forces fired on Union troops at Fort Sumter, effectively beginning the Civil War. Lincoln took several immediate actions to quell the rebellion: expanding his war powers, imposing a blockade on Confederate shipping ports, disbursing funds without the approval of Congress, and suspending habeas corpus to allow the arrest and imprisonment of thousands of suspected Confederate sympathizers without trials.

In January of 1863, more than a year and a half into the Civil War, Lincoln signed a presidential proclamation declaring that all slaves in the states still in rebellion against the Union were thereby freed. Over the course of the next several years, all states were encouraged or coerced into prohibiting human slavery as a practice.

Effects of Lincoln's election

In the election of 1860, Abraham Lincoln defeated three other challengers. Lincoln's platform was anti-slavery, though he vowed to leave it intact where it already existed. He also promised full rights to immigrants, the completion of a Pacific Railroad, free homesteads, and a protective tariff. After the election, South Carolina seceded, followed by the rest of the Deep South (Mississippi, Alabama, Georgia, Louisiana, Florida and Texas). These states established the Confederate States of America, with its capital in Montgomery, Alabama. The president of the CSA was Jefferson Davis. Outgoing US President Buchanan claimed that he had no constitutional authority to stop the secession, but upon entering office Lincoln attempted to maintain control of all Southern forts. This led to the firing on Ft. Sumter (SC) by the Confederates. As Lincoln called for aid, the Upper South (Virginia, Arkansas, North Carolina and Tennessee) seceded as well, and the CSA made Richmond, Virginia its new capital.

The Civil War

The Civil War was fought for a number of reasons, but the most important of these was the controversy about slavery. The issue of slavery touched on moral, economic, and political themes. Also, the differing geography of the North and South had caused the latter to develop an economy that they felt could only survive through slavery. The Civil War also sprang from the ongoing debate over states' rights; many in the South felt that states should have the power to nullify federal regulations and believed that the North had too much representation in Congress; and, indeed, the North had received much more federal aid for infrastructure. Finally, there was a general difference in culture between the North and South; the North was more of a dynamic and democratic society, while the South was more of a static oligarchy.

Robert E. Lee

Robert E. Lee was the commander of the Confederate Army of Northern Virginia during the Civil War. In 1861, President Lincoln offered Lee command of the Union Army, but Lee declined because his home state, Virginia, was threatening to secede from the Union. When the Confederacy was established, Lee became a senior military advisor to President Jefferson Davis. General Lee led many great battles but was unable to invade the North. He surrendered at Appomattox Courthouse in 1865, which marked the beginning of the end for the South. Only two months later, the last of the Confederate Armies surrendered.

Important battles and people of the Civil War

The Battle of Fort Sumter (1861) was the first battle of the American Civil War. Confederate troops bombarded Fort Sumter near Charleston, South Carolina, and forced the Union troops to abandon it.

The Battle of Gettysburg (1863) was a major battle during the American Civil War. It resulted in the largest number of casualties, and saw the tide turn in favor of the North.

The Battle of Appomattox Court House (1865) was one of the final battles of the America Civil War, and ended with General Robert E. Lee surrendering to General Ulysses S. Grant.

General Robert E. Lee was the commander of the Army of Northern Virginia during the American Civil War, and was eventually promoted to general-in-chief of the Confederate forces.

General Ulysses S. Grant was the commander of all Union forces during the American Civil War. He was later elected the 18th President of the United States.

Battle of Antietam and the Emancipation Proclamation

At the Battle of Antietam (MD) in September of 1862, the Confederate General Robert E. Lee went on the offensive, hoping to bring Maryland into the Confederacy, sever the channels between Washington, DC and the North, and attract the recognition of the European powers. This was the bloodiest battle of the Civil War and ended in a draw. It was after this battle that Lincoln issued his famous Emancipation Proclamation. This document freed the slaves in any area that was taken by the Union, or in areas from which slaves could enter the Union. It did not, however, free slaves in the Border States, because Lincoln wanted to maintain loyalty to the Union in these areas. The aims of the Emancipation Proclamation were three: to keep the British from assisting the South, to motivate the Northern troops and to effect a positive moral change.

States' rights and the Civil War

Advocates of states' rights believed that the powers of the individual state were equal to or greater than those of the federal government. The issue of each state, as opposed to the federal government, having sovereign authority over its citizens led to the secession of the South, which, in turn, led to the Civil War. Southerners believed they had a right to make decisions for themselves regarding slavery and taxes, among other issues. They did not think the federal government was constitutionally authorized to tell them what to do. Because Southerners believed that the power of the Union rested in each state making decisions for itself based on its self-interest, states in the South began to secede from the Union.

Tariff policies and the Civil War

Tariffs are taxes that a government levies on imported goods in order to raise funds. Because tariffs are added to foreign-made products, those products become more expensive than American-made goods. The Northern and Southern states had very different attitudes toward tariffs. Northern businessmen generally favored tariffs because they gave them an advantage over foreign companies. Southerners, on the other hand, sold most of their cotton to foreign buyers in exchange for foreign credit they could use to purchase foreign goods. But, this meant they had to buy foreign products, which cost more than domestic ones. The fact that these products were more expensive put the South at a disadvantage. Northerners and Southerners wanted the federal government to do opposing things with respect to tariffs.

The issue of trade and tariffs created significant differences between the North and South that led to the Civil War. The North had a domestic economy and viewed foreign trade as competition. When foreign goods are taxed at a higher rate, the goods become more expensive and less competitive. For this reason, Northerners argued in favor of protective tariffs. The South, on the other hand, was very dependent on imported manufactured goods from Europe. The South also exported much of its agricultural goods. For these reasons, the South was opposed to protective tariffs, which made goods more expensive for Southerners to buy. The disagreement over protective tariffs led to the Nullification Crisis of 1832 when South Carolina declared the tariffs null and void within its state borders.

Gettysburg Address

The Gettysburg Address was a speech that President Abraham Lincoln delivered in Gettysburg, Pennsylvania, during the Civil War. The speech was given to dedicate a national cemetery on the grounds of the Battle of Gettysburg. President Lincoln's speech was a comment on the ideals of democracy: liberty and freedom for all. He felt that these ideals were being threatened by the Civil War. He reminded the country that it was founded on the precept that all men are created equal and that the country fought hard to have a government of the people, by the people, and for the people. He wanted the citizens to join together to preserve the ideals of democracy.

Reconstruction Era

The Reconstruction Era in the United States began as the Civil War ended, and lasted until 1877. Its purpose was to address how the eleven states that had seceded from the Union would regain self-government and be reseated to Congress. It also focused on the Constitutional and legal status of both the former leaders of the Confederacy and the freed slaves. As Confederate states came back under the control of the U.S. Army, President Lincoln began setting up reconstructed governments in some of the states, and experimented with giving land to former slaves in others. After Lincoln's assassination in 1865, Democrat Andrew Johnson came to power and attempted to reign in the previous administration's plan for reconstruction. This action was met with fierce opposition in the Republican Congress and they rejected his terms, eventually voting to remove the civilian governments that had been established in the South and returned control to the U.S. Army. The period of Reconstruction ended at different times in different states, usually corresponding to the loss of Republican control in the state legislatures. With the Compromise of 1877, federal military intervention in the South finally ended.

Westward Expansion

America's westward expansion led to conflict and violent confrontations with Native Americans such as the Battle of Little Bighorn. In 1876, the American government ordered all Indians to relocate to reservations. Lack of compliance led to the Dawes Act in 1887, which ordered assimilation rather than separation. This act remained in effect until 1934. Reformers also forced Indian children to attend Indian Boarding Schools, where they were not allowed to speak their native language and were forced to accept Christianity. Children were often abused in these schools, and were indoctrinated to abandon their identity as Native Americans.

In 1890, the massacre at Wounded Knee, accompanied by Geronimo's surrender, led the Native Americans to work to preserve their culture rather than fight for their lands.

Political effects of slavery

Advocates of states' rights believed that the powers of the individual state were paramount to those of the federal government. The issue of each state, as opposed to the federal government, having sovereign authority over its citizens led to the secession of the South, which, in turn, led to the Civil War. Southerners believed they had a right to make decisions for themselves regarding slavery and taxes, among other issues. They did not think the federal government could tell them what to do. Because Southerners believed that the power of the Union rested in each state making decisions for itself based on its self-interest, states in the South began to secede from the Union.

Economic reasons for growth of the slave trade

Economic reasons were a major factor in the growth of the slave trade in the South before the Civil War. Plantation owners needed abundant cheap labor in order to make money growing rice, cotton, sugar, tobacco and other products they exported abroad. Slaves were basically free labor, though owners did need to feed and clothe them. Plantation owners would buy more slaves in order to grow more crops to make more money, Slavery was basically a way for plantation owners to exploit a source of labor for their own profit, but it became entrenched in the economy of the South.

Homestead Act

The US government tried many different ways to improve conditions for farmers in the West. Under the Homestead Act of 1862, farmers were sold 160 acres for $10, with the proviso that they had to improve the land within 5 years. Between the years 1865 and 1900, only one in six farms began this way. The Timber Culture Act of 1873 gave more land to farmers, with the proviso that they had to plant some trees on that land.

One thing that helped to populate the West was the completion of the Transcontinental Railroad in 1869. The Union Pacific met the Central Pacific railway at Promontory Point, Utah. In 1889, the US government opened Oklahoma for settlement, and by 1893 it was completely settled.

Territories and territorial acquisitions

The following were major territories or territorial acquisitions in the late 1700s and early 1800s:

- The Northwest Territory was established in 1787. It included all United States land west of Pennsylvania and northwest of the Ohio River, covering the present-day states of Ohio, Indiana, Illinois, Michigan, Wisconsin, and Minnesota. The United States acquired the Northwest Territory from Britain through the Treaty of Paris.
- The Southwest Territory was established in 1790. When it was admitted to the United States, it became the present-day state of Tennessee and part of the Mississippi Territory. The Southwest Territory was originally part of South Carolina, but was eventually ceded to the United States government.
- The Michigan Territory was established in 1805. It eventually became the present-day state of Michigan. The British government ceded the Michigan Territory to the United States government in 1783.
- The Louisiana Purchase was a territorial acquisition in which the United States purchased a large area of land from France in 1803. The area of land included 14 present-day states.

Southern crops during the 1800s

The most important crops grown in the South during the 1800s were cotton and tobacco. Rice, indigo, and sugar were other major cash crops for the South during this period. The South relied on agriculture much more than did the Northern states. Growing and harvesting crops requires much manpower. For this reason, Southern whites depended on slaves. This economic dependence allowed slavery to become an integral part of Southern life, which, in turn, led to sharp differences between the North and South, and, eventually, the Civil War.

Absolute and relative chronology

Chronology means arranging events in the order they occurred in time. A timeline is one common way of showing a chronology. Absolute chronology is based on a calendar. In an absolute chronology, events are located based on the day, month, or year they occurred and are organized from oldest to most recent. Relative chronology, on the other hand, is a chronology in which events are located relative to each other. The relationship of the events, rather than a calendar, is the organizational tool. A particular event is located based on when another event occurred. For example, event X occurred first, event Y occurred second, and event Z occurred third.

Geography and Culture

The Puritans

The Puritans established the colony of Massachusetts Bay in 1630. They hoped to purify the Church of England and then return to Europe with a new and improved religion. The Massachusetts Bay Puritans were more immediately successful than other fledgling colonies because they brought enough supplies, arrived in the springtime, and had good leadership (including John Winthrop). Puritans fished, cut timber for ships, and trapped fur. The local government was inextricably bound with the church; only church members were allowed to vote for the General Court (similar to the House of Burgesses), although everyone was required to pay taxes. The Puritans established a Bible Commonwealth that would last 50 years. During this time, Old Testament law was the law of the community.

There was more chance for social mobility in Massachusetts than in any other colony in America. This was mainly due to the diverse economy. As for religion, it dominated every area of an individual's life. The Puritan Church was known as the Congregational Church; at first, this was an exclusive group, but it gradually became easier to become a member. Indeed, by the mid-1600s religious fervor seemed to be waning in Massachusetts. A group called the Jeremiads warned the people that they were in danger of lapsing into atheism, but many people did not mind. Around this time, ministers began to offer half-way covenants, which gave church members partial privileges.

The Great Awakening

The Great Awakening was a religious revival in New England in the 1730s and 40s. It began in response to the growing secularism and was aided by the recent migrations into the cities, where it was easier for large crowds to form. Jonathan Edwards was one of the most famous preachers of this time. The Great Awakening was the first mass movement in America; it helped break down the divides between the various regions of the British colonies and led to the formation of some new Protestant denominations. Though the Revivalists did not directly advocate the abolition of slavery, they did suggest that there was divinity in all creation, and that therefore blacks were worthy of being converted to Christianity.

Society of the Middle Colonies

The Middle Colonies (New York, Pennsylvania, Delaware, East and West New Jersey) shared characteristics with both New England and the Southern colonies. The economy was diverse, though less so than in New England. Shipping and commerce would gradually become crucial in the port cities of Philadelphia and New York. There were plenty of slaves in the Middle Colonies, most of whom served as laborers on ships. The Dutch treated their slaves well; the English did not. People in these colonies tended to have a healthier lifestyle than their neighbors to the south, and therefore they tended to live longer. The diverse economy made social mobility possible, though large landowners were for the most part entrenched in positions of power.

Louisiana Purchase

The area acquired by the Louisiana Purchase included the present states of Arkansas, Missouri, Iowa, Oklahoma, Kansas, and Nebraska. Parts of Minnesota, North Dakota, South Dakota, New Mexico, Montana, Wyoming, Colorado, and Louisiana were included as well. The Louisiana Purchase doubled the area of the United States at the time. The acquired area is marked by the dark border in the map below.

Abolitionist movement

The abolitionist movement of the 19th century was a social movement to end slavery and emancipate slaves. Slavery was an integral part of the American South. Most abolitionists were Northerners. They considered slavery a moral disease that threatened the Union. Abolitionists worked through political channels to free slaves and end the system of slavery. Some worked to help escaped slaves on the Underground Railroad. The turning point for the movement came in 1860 when Abraham Lincoln, who opposed the spread of slavery, became president of the United States.

Life in Southern Colonies

The social lives of the Southern colonists were filled with dancing, card-playing, cotillions, hunts, and large community dinners. Southerners were considered to be very optimistic in temperament, in contrast to their more dour Northern counterparts. It was extremely difficult to move up in the social hierarchy in the South; the richer colonists generally took the best land and thus were able to maintain their position in the economy and in the government, as the poor had to move away from the towns to find farmland. Because farming was the only available occupation, there were not any venues for ambitious men to distinguish themselves. North Carolina was generally considered to be the state with the least social stratification.

In the early days of the Southern colonies, most people lived on small farms. Although they made up a tiny part of the population, the owners of the coastal plantations wielded enormous power. These aristocrats typically grew a single crop on their lands: in North Carolina, Virginia, and Maryland, tobacco was the cash crop, while the large growers in South Carolina and Georgia favored rice and indigo. Plantations, like the feudal manors of the past, were almost totally self-sufficient units, although the owners imported most of their luxury items from England. The Southern colonies had the closest ties with England, mainly because England provided the market for their tobacco; crops grown in the colonies were sold back in England by agents (known as factors).

Expansion into Texas

In 1821, Mexico received its independence from Spain. Mexico sold Texan lands to Americans, yet these people were still required to live under Mexican civil law (for one thing, people had to convert

- 28 -

to Catholicism). In 1832, however, Santa Anna led a coup in Mexico and decided to crack down on the Texans. This led to the Texas Revolution of 1836, in which Texan General William Travis' men were massacred by the forces of Santa Anna at the Alamo, in which both Davy Crockett and Jim Bowie were killed. After suffering some other defeats the Texans, led by Sam Houston, finally defeated Santa Anna at the Battle of San Jacinto in 1836 and he was forced below the Rio Grande. Nevertheless, Texas was not made part of the US, mainly because the issue of slavery was so contentious at the time. It would not be annexed and admitted into the Union until 1845.

U.S expansion to Salt Lake City, Oregon, and California

The territory of Oregon became more important to the US government as fur-trapping became a lucrative industry. Oregon was also known to contain rich farmland. As for California, its natural bounty had been described by whalers since the 1820s. In the 1840s, whole families (including the ill-fated Donner party) began to migrate there. Around this time the Church of Jesus Christ of Latter-day Saints, otherwise known as the Mormon Church, was founded by Joseph Smith. Among the beliefs espoused by the Mormons were polygamy, communalism and the abolition of slavery. After Smith's death, the Mormons were led by Brigham Young and settled in what is now Salt Lake City. Meanwhile, in 1848 gold was discovered in a California stream, generating still more excitement over the economic potential of the West.

Women's rights movement

The women's rights movement began in the 1840s with leaders including Elizabeth Cady Stanton, Ernestine Rose and Lucretia Mott. Later, in 1869, the National Woman Suffrage Association, fighting for women's right to vote, came into being. It was led by Susan B. Anthony, Ernestine Rose and Elizabeth Cady Stanton. In 1848 in Seneca Falls, the first women's rights convention was held, with about three hundred attendees. The Seneca Falls Convention brought to the floor the issue that women could not vote or run for office. The convention produced a "Declaration of Sentiments" which outlined a plan for women to attain the rights they deserved. Frederick Douglass supported the women's rights movement, as well as the abolition movement. In fact, women's rights and abolition movements often went hand-in-hand through this time period.

Confederate States of America during the Civil War

The area that made up the Confederate States of America during the Civil War included the states of Virginia, Georgia, North Carolina, South Carolina, Mississippi, Florida, Alabama, Louisiana, Texas, Arkansas, and Tennessee. These are all the states south of the thick line on the map below.

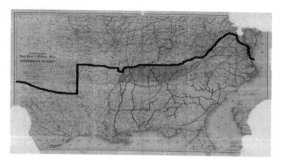

Temperance movement of the 19th century

The temperance movement of the 19th century was a social movement, led mostly by women, to discourage the consumption of alcohol. As the movement gained ground in the mid-1800s, it

- 29 -

changed from a purely social movement advocating moderation in the consumption of alcohol to a political movement that was successful in getting the government to regulate the sale of alcohol. The 18th Amendment to the Constitution established Prohibition, which made alcohol illegal in this country. Through this lens, the temperance movement of the 19th century was very successful in achieving its goals and had a significant impact on life in the United States. (The 18th Amendment was repealed by the 21st Amendment in 1933 and is the only constitutional amendment to have been repealed.)

Panama Canal

The Spanish-American War had demonstrated that the US needed a Latin American canal in order to become a major naval power. At that time, however, their hands were tied by the Clayton-Bulwer Treaty of 1850, which had stated that neither the US nor Britain would build a canal in Latin America without the other. Fortunately for the US, the British were distracted by the Boer War in South Africa and thus were willing to sign the Hay-Pauncefote Treaty in 1901, allowing the US to go it alone. Many in the US, including Roosevelt, wanted to build the canal in Nicaragua because it has a number of lakes that could be connected, and because it is mostly flat. Others lobbied for Panama, pointing out that a French contractor had already started work on a canal there and that Panama was narrower than Nicaragua.

Once Roosevelt finally secured the building supplies and the land to construct the Panama Canal, the brutal and dangerous work began. In order to prevent malaria the US paved streets, drained swamps, and built houses so that the workers would not have to sleep in tents. Nevertheless, the workdays were long and the pay was low. In the end, the canal cost about $400 million; it was finished in 1913, but did not open until the next year. Roosevelt's visit to Panama made him the first president to leave the US during his term. In 1920, a guilty Democratic Congress gave Colombia $25 million. At present, about 12,000 ships go through the canal every year and it takes about 8 hours to get from one end to the other.

Susan B. Anthony

In her twenties, Anthony was a schoolteacher and then a headmistress. Observing that men teachers' wages were four times those of women inspired her to fight for equal pay. Before the Civil War, she worked for temperance and antislavery movements. Reading of the first National Women's Rights Convention in 1850 and Horace Greeley's admiration of a speech by Lucy Stone, Anthony was inspired by Stone's speech to dedicate her life to women's rights, later meeting Greeley and Stone in 1852. In 1851, after a convention's denying her admission for being female, Anthony organized America's first women's state temperance society with Elizabeth Cady Stanton. Thereafter they crossed the country speaking together for women's equal treatment. They founded the National Woman Suffrage Association (NWSA) in 1869. Anthony's 1872 arrest, trial, and conviction for voting illegally gave her an even bigger audience for women's suffrage. Anthony copublished The History of Women's Suffrage (1884–1887). In 1890, she engineered NWSA's merger with Stone's AWSA, forming the NAWSA.

W.E.B. Du Bois's work as civil rights activist

Du Bois was the foremost intellectual and political activist for African-Americans in the 20th century's first half and was called "The Father of Pan-Africanism." He and educator Booker T. Washington collaborated on ideas for solutions to political disenfranchisement and segregation, and on organizing the "Negro Exhibition" showing black contributions to American society at Paris's 1900 Exposition Universelle. In 1905 he cofounded the Niagara Movement, championing free speech, voting, leadership, and antiracist ideals. Cofounder William Trotter felt whites should be excluded. Du Bois disagreed and cofounded the National Association for the Advancement of Colored People (NAACP) in 1909 where races could unite for civil rights. He left his faculty position at Atlanta University and became NAACP's publications director in 1910, publishing Harlem Renaissance writers Langston Hughes and Jean Toomer. Becoming more radical as NAACP became more institutionalized, Du Bois suggested black separatism as an economic policy in the 1930s and returned to teaching at Atlanta University. He corresponded with NAACP member Albert Einstein, who called racism "America's worst disease" in 1946.

Economic geography of the United States

As a current superpower, the United States has one of the most advanced economies in the world. Like Canada, the United States contains many deposits of natural resources. For instance, the North American realm has more coal reserves than any other. The spatial organization of regional agricultural production in the United States exists within the framework of a modified Von Thunen model, with the "megalopolis" of New England at its center, and belts of specialized activity extending westward. Though the manufacturing sector is less important in a postindustrial economy, this type of activity is still practiced in the United States, and tends to cluster around several urban-industrial nodes, especially within the Manufacturing Belt (located in the Northeast United States). Increased mechanization and advancements in technology have eliminated many "blue-collar" jobs in this region. Most laborers in the U.S. workforce are employed in quaternary economic activity. States offering noneconomic amenities (such as weather and proximity to urban centers and universities) have experienced higher levels of growth than other regions.

Cultures of the United States

The United States supports a diverse culture, as it was formed from groups of native races as well as large numbers of immigrants. It functioned for a period under British rule. The United States broke from British rule via violent revolution. Agriculture, industries and technology all play a large part in the United States economy. The United States in general supports a high standard of living and a high level of development, and supports trade with countries throughout the world.

Climate of the United States

The U.S. has a vast distribution of geographical features, with mountain ranges in both east and west, stretches of fertile plains through the center, and large lakes and waterways. Many of these areas were shaped by glaciers, which also deposited highly fertile soil.

Because it is so large, the US experiences several varieties of climate, including continental climates with four seasons in median areas, tropical climates in the southern part of the US, and arctic climes in the far north. Human intervention has greatly influenced the productivity of agricultural regions, and many areas have been reshaped to accommodate easier, more economical transportation.

The Battle Hymn of the Republic

The Battle Hymn of the Republic was written by Julia Ward Howe. The hymn used the music from the song *John Brown's Body*, but Howe's more famous lyrics quickly became the words most commonly associated with the tune. The song, which makes reference to the Biblical final judgment of the wicked, was sung as a campfire song by Union soldiers during the Civil War, and became a prominent American patriotic song.

Transcendentalism

Transcendentalism was a religious and philosophical movement that came about during the first half of the 19th century. It began as a general protest against the state of the culture and society, and in particular against the intellectualism popular at the time. At the most basic levels, the Transcendentalists believed that people were inherently good, as was nature in general. They also believed that certain institutions, primarily organized religion and politics, corrupted the purity of the individual and, as such, should be avoided. Transcendentalism held to the view that religion was not subject to empirical proof, and could be based simply on one's own personal individual experience.

Government and Citizenship

Magna Carta and the English Bill of Rights

The Magna Carta was an English charter that was put into law in 1215 and then revised in 1297. It was the first document to limit the powers of the English king (King John) and grant liberties to certain citizens. It also mandated that free persons could only be punished according to the law of the land. The Magna Carta contributed to the development of constitutional law and inspired the creation of the United States Constitution.

The English Bill of Rights was passed by English Parliament in 1689. It prevented the king from suspending laws and forced royalty to abide by the laws of parliament. It influenced the United States Bill of Rights, specifically the right to trial by jury and the prohibition of excessive bail and cruel and unusual punishment.

Federalist Papers and Anti-Federalist Papers

Major Federalist leaders included Alexander Hamilton, John Jay and James Madison. They wrote a series of letters, called the Federalist Papers, aimed at convincing the states to ratify the Constitution. These were published in New York papers. Anti-Federalists included Thomas Jefferson and Patrick Henry. They argued against the Constitution as it was originally drafted in arguments called the Anti-Federalist Papers. The final compromise produced a strong central government controlled by checks and balances. A Bill of Rights was also added, becoming the first ten amendments to the Constitution. These amendments protected rights such as freedom of speech, freedom of religion, and other basic rights. Aside from various amendments added throughout the years, the United States Constitution has remained unchanged.

Separation of powers

Separation of powers means that the government has three branches: legislative, executive, and judicial. Through a system of checks and balances, these branches work together and none is allowed to become too powerful. The separation of powers is granted in the U.S. Constitution. The Constitution states that Congress has the "legislative powers herein granted" and lists the actions in Article I, Section 8, that Congress is allowed to take. The next section lists those actions that are prohibited for Congress to take. Article II describes the powers of the executive branch, including the president, and Article III gives judicial power to the Supreme Court.

Republicanism and individual rights

Republicanism is a governing philosophy that emphasizes individual liberty, inalienable rights, and popular sovereignty. It rejects inherited power and government corruption. Republicanism and democracy are not the same. In a democracy, the majority can vote to remove rights from a minority group. However, in a republic, every person is granted certain inalienable rights that cannot be taken away by anyone. The Constitution protected the rights of individuals by incorporating certain republican elements. The Constitution:

- Created a senate that was controlled by the states.
- Established an electoral college to elect the president rather than relying on a straight popular vote.
- Preserved the sovereignty of individual states.
- Required a super majority to amend the Constitution.

Individual rights are held by the citizens of a country, and cannot be taken away by any person or group without due process. The Constitution enumerates the individual rights of U.S. citizens within the Bill of Rights.

Changing the U.S. Constitution

The U.S. Constitution can be changed but only through the difficult process of amendment. The first step is for a bill to pass both houses of Congress--the Senate and the House of Representatives--by a two-thirds majority in each. This is no easy task. Next, the bill must go to the states for approval. The amendment must be approved by three-fourths of the states. Usually, this is done in the state legislatures by a simple majority vote. If three-fourths of the states approve the amendment, it becomes part of the U.S. Constitution. The president of the United States has no formal role in the amendment process. Only 27 amendments have been added in the history of the U.S. Constitution.

13th, 14th, and 15th amendments

The 13th, 14th and 15th amendments were passed during the Reconstruction era after the Civil War ended. The 13th amendment to the U.S. Constitution freed all slaves and legally forbade slavery in the United States. Slaves were freed without giving monetary compensation to the slaveholders. The fact that slavery was made illegal has had a huge impact on life in the United States, altering the societal composition of Southern states as well as some border states.

The 14th amendment declared that all persons born or naturalized (except Native American Indians) were U.S. citizens and that all citizens were entitled to equal rights regardless of race. Most of the Confederate states were forced to comply based on the Military Reconstruction Act. The amendment fell short of giving black men the right to vote but paved the way for the 15th amendment. It angered women's rights activists because it made the right to vote a male right. The major impact of the 14th amendment was that human rights were granted at the state as well as the national level through the "due process clause."

The 15th amendment granted black men the right to vote. Like the 14th amendment, it passed because Confederate states were forced to comply based on the Military Reconstruction Act. Women's rights activists opposed the amendment because it granted the right to vote to males only. Women weren't granted the right to vote until the passage of the 19th amendment. The 13th, 14th and 15th amendments had a huge impact on life in the United States because they put an end to the era of slavery and were the first steps in giving freedom and equal rights to black people at the state and national levels.

Marbury v. Madison

Marbury v. Madison was the first Supreme Court judgment that supported the federal system of government. In 1803 this landmark case established the principle of judicial review, which means the judiciary can determine that a law is unconstitutional. The principle of judicial review gives more power to the U.S. Constitution than to the legislature, because laws created and passed by the legislature may still be deemed unconstitutional. William Marbury was denied his claim regarding his appointment as a justice of the peace because the U.S. Supreme Court determined that the statute on which he based his claim was unconstitutional. This case helped define the system of checks and balances.

Landmark Supreme Court cases

The Supreme Court led by John Marshall is credited with increasing the power of the national government over that of the states. This court also gave the judicial branch more power and prestige, notably in the case of Marbury v. Madison (1803). Marshall was known as an arch-Federalist, and as a loose interpreter of the Constitution. In the case McCullough v. Maryland (1819), the court ruled that a national bank is allowed by the Constitution, and that states cannot tax a federal agency. In the case of Gibbons v. Ogden (1824), the right of Congress to regulate interstate commerce was reaffirmed, and indeed federal regulation of just about anything was made possible. In Fletcher v. Peck (1810), the sanctity of contracts was asserted; this case also established the right of the Supreme Court to declare state laws unconstitutional.

Unalienable rights

The term unalienable rights refers to the fundamental rights that are guaranteed to people naturally instead of by law. People have certain natural rights, and laws cannot take them away. The Declaration of Independence stated that these unalienable rights are: "life, liberty, and the pursuit of happiness." The Bill of Rights, which is the first 10 amendments to the Constitution, lists religious freedom, freedom of speech and of the press, and the right to assemble and petition as additional unalienable rights that people possess.

Rights guaranteed by the Bill of Rights

The Bill of Rights is composed of the first ten amendments to the U.S. Constitution. The ten amendments were passed on December 15, 1791. The rights that are protected by each amendment are listed here:

- Freedom of religion, speech, press, peaceable assembly, and government petition.
- The right to bear arms.
- Protection from the quartering of soldiers in private homes except by law during wartime.
- Protection from unreasonable search and seizure.
- Due process and protection from double jeopardy and self-incrimination.
- The right of the accused to a speedy, public criminal trial before an impartial jury.
- The right to a civil trial by jury in accord with common law.
- Protection from cruel and unusual punishment and excessive fines and bail.
- The preservation of rights not mentioned.
- The preservation of the rights of states and individuals.

Becoming a naturalized citizen of the United States

Naturalization is the acquisition of citizenship of a country by a person who was not previously a citizen of that country. There are several ways to qualify for citizenship through naturalization in the United States. A legal resident alien may apply for US citizenship after living as a permanent resident of the US for at least 5 years, or 3 years while married to a US citizen. Alternatively, serving a designated period of time in the US Armed Forces qualifies one to apply for citizenship after only 1 year of permanent residency. Once one of these qualifications is met, a person may apply and will be required to pass a citizenship test.

Free speech

Freedom of speech is one of the rights protected by the Bill of Rights, which is the first 10 amendments to the U.S. Constitution. Freedom of speech is crucial to a democratic society because each person is allowed to say whatever he or she thinks, even something negative about the government of the country. This freedom allows critics of governmental policies to voice their concerns without fear of reprisals. Having open discourse about the policies and laws of the country is one of the hallmarks of a free and democratic society.

James Monroe

In the election of 1816, the Democrat-Republican James Monroe defeated the last Federalist candidate, Rufus King, by a landslide. The Federalist opposition to the War of 1812 doomed the party to extinction. Monroe's early term was not without its problems, however. A mild depression caused by over-speculation on western lands led to the Panic of 1819, and began a 20-year boom-bust cycle. These problems were exacerbated by the Second Bank of the United States; the Bank's pressure on the so-called "wildcat" banks to foreclose on properties, as well as the unwillingness of the Bank to loan money, made it very unpopular. The nationalism generated by the War of 1812 was damaged by these economic travails.

In 1823, President James Monroe formulated a foreign policy which is known today as the Monroe Doctrine. In his annual address to Congress, Monroe indicated that the Old World (namely Europe) and the New World (namely the United States) were distinct entities with distinct systems, and should therefore exist as separate spheres. His statement included four main points:

- the United States would not participate in conflicts within or between European nations
- the United States officially recognized and would not interfere with existing colonies in the New World
- the Western Hemisphere was off limits for future colonization
- any endeavor by a European power to influence any nation in the Western Hemisphere would be considered a hostile act against the United States.

Though the Monroe Doctrine was militarily unsustainable at the time of its formulation, as the U.S. emerged as a global power in the 1870's, the Monroe Doctrine came to be viewed as a geopolitical definition of the country's sphere of influence as the entire Western Hemisphere.

Elizabeth Cady Stanton

Elizabeth Cady Stanton was the author of the Declaration of Rights of Women. She spent her life working for the rights of women, especially the right to vote. Working with Lucretia Mott, she organized the Seneca Falls Women's Rights Convention, where she wrote the Declaration of Rights. She pushed the assembly to adopt a resolution calling for women to gain the right to vote. Stanton was an important thinker in the women's rights movement, in addition to being a wife and mother of seven children.

Economics, Science, Technology, and Society

Plantation system

The plantation system was the main method of agricultural production in the South. Plantations were large farms that had 20 or more slaves and produced one staple crop (i.e., rice, cotton, tobacco, or sugar). Much financial gain could be made by growing and selling these crops. However, such crops were very labor-intensive to grow and harvest. Plantation owners made the system profitable by having slaves who were basically free labor. Plantation owners thus owned the land, the tools, and the labor force. This allowed them to make more money.

Transatlantic slave trade

The transatlantic slave trade was the industry of buying and selling slaves carried over from the African continent during the 16th through 19th centuries. The slaves were mostly West Africans kidnapped by rival African tribes and sold to European traders who transported them by ship to the New World. Slaves were a valuable commodity because, once purchased, a slave represented free labor for life. The American colonies, and later the United States, received a relatively small percentage of the slaves transported to the new world (only about 6%), the majority of whom were sold in the agricultural South. Southerners eventually came to depend on slaves to maintain their farms and plantations, ensuring continued demand for the slave trade.

Economic reasons for rapid industrialization

Rapid industrialization in the United States occurred during the Industrial Revolution of the 19th century (1820-1870). The Embargo Act of 1807 stopped the export of American goods and made the import of goods very difficult. Trade essentially came to a halt. This meant that the United States needed to become more independent, and the way to do so was to become more industrial. Manufacturing began to expand, and the government protected American manufacturing by passing a protective tariff on foreign-made goods. As factories and industries grew, domestic goods could be produced more quickly and cheaply.

Transportation systems and urbanization

The Industrial Revolution had brought many industries and factories to cities. The growth of the transportation systems, mainly railroad and steamships, led to urbanization by increasing trade and making it possible to bring raw materials from the West to the factories in the East. This enabled the industries and factories to be successful and to grow. People wanted to be a part of these growing industries. Countless Americans moved from their farms to the cities because that is where the economic opportunities were.

Free enterprise system

The term "free enterprise system" refers to the capitalist system of economics. In a capitalist society, businesses are privately owned and goods are traded in markets. In a purely free enterprise, or market, system, everything can be owned privately. The government does not own anything or interfere in the private sector in any way. In a free market system, the individual can make his or her own economic choices without government involvement. People can choose what to produce, how to produce, how many to produce, and for whom to produce. Business owners can decide how to structure their businesses. Competition between companies is central to the free enterprise system.

Impact of the Mississippi River

The Mississippi River was acquired by the United States in the Louisiana Purchase and is the largest river in North America. People live near rivers because they provide water for agriculture and a means to transport goods for economic gain. When the United States gained control over the Mississippi, many people moved westward and settled on its banks. During the 19th century, steamboats traveled up and down the river, bringing goods to the people who lived along its banks and taking exports to sell in other places. New Orleans developed as a major port city, and other cities, such as St. Louis, grew and thrived because of their location on the banks of the Mississippi River.

Technological innovations in the 19th century

Technological innovations in the 19th century were instrumental in changing the way goods were manufactured. The most important innovation may well have been the cotton gin. Eli Whitney's invention made it possible to separate cotton seeds from the fiber of the plant. Previous to his invention, this task had been very time-consuming and labor- intensive. Because of the cotton gin, the South was able to send more cotton fiber to the North to be made into cloth. New processes for manufacturing cloth and the invention of the sewing machine enabled the textile industry to flourish in the North. The cotton gin is an example of the new way in which machines were used to manufacture goods at a much faster rate than humans could do on their own.

Industrialization in the 19th century

The Industrial Revolution in the United States lasted from 1820-1870. During that time, machines and factories took over the production of goods. These technologies allowed goods to be produced at a much faster rate so businesses could sell more products and make more money. Railroads lines were being expanded, so goods more easily could travel across the country to new markets. Industrialization changed life in the United States because the country shifted from an agricultural economy to an industrial economy. People moved to cities where the factories were and no longer worked on family farms. The Industrial Revolution turned the United States into a modern country.

Social Studies Practice Test #1

1. The three branches of government established by the US Constitution are divisions of the:
    a. Federal government
    b. Municipal government
    c. Regional government
    d. State government

2. The legislative branch of government is comprised of:
    a. Congress
    b. The House of Representatives
    c. State legislatures
    d. Senators

3. Broad Constructionists interpret the Constitution:
    a. Based on the Chief Justice's legal training
    b. In a manner that reflects the values of the justices
    c. Regarding the amendments as more important
    d. Valuing the states over the federal government

4. The first amendment guarantees all below except:
    a. Freedom of assembly
    b. The right to bear arms
    c. Freedom of the press
    d. The right to speak freely

5. Filibuster is a legislative procedure:
    a. Used to enact legislation quickly
    b. Used in the Supreme Court
    c. Used in the Senate
    d. Used by the President

6. Isolationism is a doctrine that says the US is best served staying out of foreign affairs and disputes. After the Revolutionary War, the US tried to maintain its isolationist strategy until:
    a. The Civil War
    b. The French and Indian War
    c. The Vietnam War
    d. World War I

7. Which list of events is in the correct chronological order?

a.
* French and Indian War
* American Revolution
* French Revolution
* War of 1812

c.
French and Indian War
* French Revolution
* War of 1812
* American Revolution

b.
* American Revolution
* French Revolution
* War of 1812
* French and Indian War

d.
French and Indian War
* French Revolution
* War of 1812
* American Revolution

8. The temperance movement in the US was related to:

   a. Abolition
   b. Civil disobedience
   c. Pacifism
   d. Revolution

9. Which of the following Supreme Court cases maintained the "separate but equal" practice of treatment toward racial minorities?

   a. Brown vs. Board of Education
   b. Marbury vs. Madison
   c. Plessy vs. Fergusson
   d. Roe vs. Wade

10. Westward migration during the 1800's in the US was catalyzed by:

   a. Overpopulation in the Northeastern US
   b. Precursors to interstate highways
   c. Potential economic opportunity
   d. Vigilantism by native peoples

11. Which of the following influenced the US Bill of Rights?

   a. The Magna Carta
   b. Martin Luther's 95 Theses
   c. Plato's Republic
   d. King James Bible

12. The US is a republic This means:

   a. Citizens vote directly on legislation
   b. Citizens elect representatives to voice their opinions
   c. Citizens elect a single leader to make decisions for the country
   d. Republicans run Congress

13. The Trail of Tears was:

   a. The forced removal of British soldiers after the American Revolution
   b. The forced evacuation of Cherokee peoples into Oklahoma
   c. The forced evacuation of freed slaves from the South after the Civil War
   d. The tears of Betsy Ross while she sewed the first American flag

14. Which of the following divided the North and South before the Civil War?

    a. The Louisiana Purchase
    b. The Mason-Dixon Line
    c. The Mississippi River
    d. The Continental Divide

15. The colony originally called New Amsterdam is now known as the state of:

    a. Delaware
    b. New York
    c. North Carolina
    d. Virginia

16. The Roanoke Colony:

    a. Provided much evidence regarding colonial culture
    b. Is also known as "the Lost Colony"
    c. Befriended many native peoples
    d. Established corn and wheat cultivation in the Americas

17. Lewis and Clark are known for exploring which region?

    a. Appalachia
    b. The Florida Keys
    c. The Pacific Northwest
    d. The Baja Peninsula of California

18. North American colonists grew cash crops, such as tobacco and cotton, primarily in what region?

    a. The New England Colonies
    b. The Central Plains
    c. The Southern Colonies
    d. The Wild West

19. Trade of rum, molasses, and slaves was among which three locales?

    a. Africa, Canada, England
    b. Africa, New England, West Indies
    c. Africa, Canada, India
    d. Amsterdam, Jamaica, South Africa

20. Modern, Federal Income Tax is an example of:

    a. Congressional taxation
    b. Presidential taxation
    c. Progressive taxation
    d. Represented taxation

21. A Writ of Habeas Corpus is a Latin phrase that translates literally to, "[We command] that you have the body." Prior to the American Revolution, English Parliament implemented this legal practice for trials in courts of law. The Habeas Corpus requirement is one right guaranteed to a defendant accused of committing a crime. Based on what you know about American civil liberties, as enumerated in the Bills of Rights, what does a Writ of Habeas Corpus ensure during a trial in a court of law in the US?

    a. That in a murder trial, the victim's body must be completely intact
    b. That a trial may not be held unless the accused is present
    c. That the accuser must be present to sentence the defendant
    d. That the judge must see the defendant before the trial begins

22. The Emancipation Proclamation resulted in:

    a. Slaves in Southern states immediately being freed
    b. Slaves in Union-controlled states being freed
    c. No new slaves being traded or purchased in the US
    d. Blacks given rights equal to whites

23. The industrial revolution was influenced by which of the following?

    a. Decrease in immigration
    b. Technological innovations
    c. Child labor restrictions
    d. Native American reconciliation

24. The House of Commons in English Parliament is similar to what entity in American Government?

    a. The House of Lords
    b. The House of Representatives
    c. The Presidential Cabinet
    d. The Supreme Court

25. Which box contains all the features of the rebel states during the Civil War?

a.		c.	
	Abolition Blue Uniforms Federal Governance Northern States		Abolition Blue Uniforms Federal Governance Northern States

b.		d.	
	Favored Slavery Grey Uniforms States Rights Southern States		No Stance on Slavery Grey Uniforms States Rights Southern States

26. Which of the following is true about the Gettysburg Address?

    a. Lincoln delivered the address at the onset of the Civil War.
    b. Emphasizes liberty as a founding principle of the US
    c. Was delivered at the Union's capital
    d. Gives the Rebels permission to leave the Union

27. Congressional districts are based on:

   a. Percentage of free men in a state
   b. Population density
   c. Presidential appointment
   d. Two representatives per state

28. Which of the founding fathers largely influenced the strength of the Federal Government?

   a. Aaron Burr
   b. Alexander Hamilton
   c. Thomas Jefferson
   d. John Hancock

29. McCullough vs. Maryland was a landmark Supreme Court case in which the state of Maryland was prohibited from imposing a tax on currency not issued by the state of Maryland: The decision sets a precedent for what principle?

   a. Federal property taxes
   b. Federally regulated currency
   c. States rights
   d. Printing currency on special paper

30. The French Revolution differs from the American Revolution by which of the following aspects?

   a. Peaceful demonstration
   b. Popular vote
   c. Violent deposition of the monarchy
   d. Philosophical ideology

31. Uncle Tom's Cabin by Harriet Beecher Stowe depicted the harsh life of slaves before the Civil War. Of the following novel titles, which likely contained a pro-slavery stance?

   a. The African-American Experience
   b. Huckleberry Finn
   c. Narrative Life of Frederick Douglas
   d. The Planter's Northern Bride

32. The "Underground Railroad" was primarily:

   a. A route for abolitionists to smuggle weapons
   b. A route for slave owners to traffic slaves
   c. A means for slaves to travel to free states
   d. A strategy for state control of railway construction

33. Which of the following differences between North and South during the Civil War was prominent in Lincoln's Gettysburg Address?

   a. State vs. federal dominance
   b. Slavery vs. abolition
   c. Agrarian vs. industrial dependence
   d. Urban vs. rural development

34. Which of the following contains congruous principals in the US between 1850 and 1920?

a.
| Slavery |
| Prohibition |
| Suffrage |

c.
| Abolition |
| Prohibition |
| States Rights |

b.
| Abolition |
| Prohibition |
| Suffrage |

d.
| Slavery |
| Prohibition |
| Municipal Rights |

35. John Locke was a philosopher who influenced the founding fathers of the US. His essays, "A Letter Concerning Toleration" (1689) and "The Second Treatise On Civil Government" (1690), promoted separation of church and state and the rights of the individual. These principals are reflected in which of the following in the US?

    a. The Bill of Rights
    b. Checks and Balances
    c. The US Senate
    d. The Oath of Presidential Office

36. The religious philosophy Thomas Jefferson embraced was called:

    a. Atheism
    b. Authoritarianism
    c. Deism
    d. Polytheism

37. Which of the following is protected based on the principal of freedom of speech?

    a. City council decisions
    b. A pamphlet distributed by the Ku Klux Klan
    c. Martial law during a disaster
    d. State income tax

38. Colonial Puritans valued hard work and individual responsibility. These characteristics are evident in what aspect of the US economy?

    a. Free-market capitalism
    b. Income taxes
    c. Labor unions
    d. Welfare benefits

39. The concept of checks and balances is evident in which of the following?

    a. Federal judiciary appeals
    b. Presidential veto
    c. States rights
    d. The House and the Senate

40. The precedent for the two-term limit for the US Presidency was established by:
   a. Abraham Lincoln
   b. Alexander Hamilton
   c. George Washington
   d. Thomas Jefferson

41. George Washington's farewell address urged future Americans to:
   a. Abolish slavery
   b. Avoid foreign alliances
   c. Encourage political party formation
   d. Promote states rights

Questions 42 & 43 pertain to the following graph:

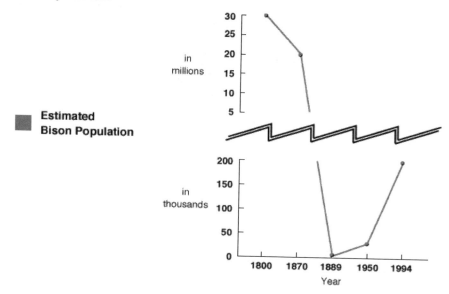

Bison Population

42. From 1800 to 1994, the Bison population in the US has:
   a. Decreased from 30 million to 200
   b. Stayed roughly the same
   c. Decreased from 30 million to 200,000
   d. Increased steadily

43. With what trend in American history did the bison population decreased to almost zero?
   a. Construction of railroads in the southeastern US
   b. The Civil War
   c. The French and Indian War
   d. Westward colonization

- 45 -

Question 44 pertains to the following map:

Largest Cities, 1900

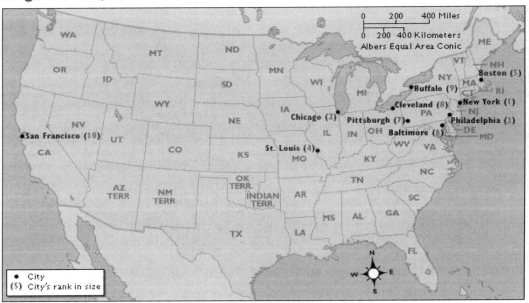

44. Which city is ranked 6th most populated?

    a. Baltimore
    b. Boston
    c. Buffalo
    d. Philadelphia

Questions 45-48 pertain to the following map:

Early European Settlements

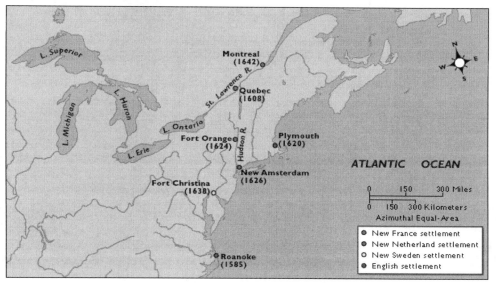

45. Which of the following is true about European colonization of the Americas?

  a. France dominated early colonization
  b. England dominated early colonization
  c. Scandinavians did not colonize to the Americas
  d. Western European countries were equally represented in the Colonies

46. What geographic feature is shared by most of the colonies?

  a. Colonies were settled based on oceanic currents
  b. Colonies were settled in comfortable climates
  c. Colonies were settled on rocky areas
  d. Colonies were settled in ports

47. Which country had the first settlement in North America?

  a. Amsterdam
  b. The Netherlands
  c. France
  d. England

48. During which century did Colonists establish the first permanent settlement in North America?

  a. 14th century
  b. 15th century
  c. 16th century
  d. 17th century

Answer Key and Explanations for Social Studies Test #1

TEKS Standard §113.20(b)(3) and (15)(D)

1. A: The US Constitution specifies three branches of federal government. The legislative branch is comprised of Congress, and Congress is comprised of the House of Representatives and the Senate.

TEKS Standard §113.20(b)(15)(D)

2. A: The US Constitution specifies three branches of federal government. The legislative branch is comprised of Congress, and Congress is comprised of the House of Representatives and the Senate.

TEKS Standard §113.20(b)(18)(A)

3. B: Loose/Broad constructionist Supreme Court Justices interprets the Constitution as a malleable document and subject to interpretation relevant to the Justices' experience and legal precedent. Decisions made by broad constructionist Justices are sometimes accused of "legislation from the bench," meaning Justices may change laws, a job supposedly given only to Congress. Broad constructionists view themselves as watchdogs for ensuring the Constitutionality of laws passed by Congress.

TEKS Standard §113.20(b)(16)

4. B: The first amendment to the Constitution states, "Congress shall make no law respecting an establishment of religion, or prohibiting the free exercise thereof; or abridging the freedom of speech or of the press; or the right of the people peaceably to assemble, and to petition the Government for a redress of grievances." The right to bear arms is guaranteed by the second amendment: "A well regulated Militia, being necessary to the security of a free State, the right of the people to keep and bear Arms, shall not be infringed."

TEKS Standard §113.20(b)(15)(D)

5. C: A filibuster is a legislative practice outlined in the Constitution that may be used by a Senator to "wear out" his opponents, so to speak. Filibuster is threatened, but rarely used. Filibuster may be stopped by a three-fifths majority of Senators.

TEKS Standard §113.20(b)(5)(E)

6. D: George Washington warned against potential pit-falls he foresaw in the future of the US: political factions, foreign allegiances that might compromise the sovereignty of the US, and too much state control, among others. The avoidance of foreign allegiances resulted in isolationism being adopted as a practice until World War I. The US, in large part, stayed out of international conflict until World War I.

TEKS Standard §113.20(b)(1)(B)

7. A: The French and Indian War (Seven Years War) 1754-1763

American Revolution 1775–1783
French Revolution 1789–1799
The War of 1812 -1815

TEKS Standard §113.20(b)(24)(B)

8. A: The movement for abolition was linked with the movement for temperance due to the triangle slave trade of sugar & molasses, rum, and slaves. The temperance movement began with the aim to eliminate hard liquor, not wine and beer.

TEKS Standard §113.20(b)(18)

9. C: Plessy vs. Fergusson (1896) was a landmark Supreme Court case that prolonged civil rights discrimination against racial minorities. Homer Plessy challenged segregation on a railway car owned by John Howard Ferguson in Louisiana. The court ruled if facilities were equal for both races, segregation was legal.

TEKS Standard §113.20(b)(1)(A) and (6)

10. C: Because land was free or very inexpensive, and the Federal Government was giving monetary incentives to expand westward (The Homestead Act gave away over 800 million acres of land from 1862-1900 to anyone establishing a homestead at which to live for a minimum of 5 years), railroads and exploration were the driving forces.

TEKS Standard §113.20(b)(15)(A)

11. A: The Magna Carta (1215) is thought by historians to be the first recognition of individual rights, the major concept put forth in the Bill of Rights. Habeas Corpus and due legal process are manifestations of those individual rights identified in the Magna Carta that exist today in the Bill of Rights.

TEKS Standard §113.20(b)(15)

12. B: The US is a republic, meaning individuals directly elect representatives to voice their opinions in democratic processes and procedures. In a true democracy, individual citizens would debate and vote on legislation and policies.

TEKS Standard §113.20(b)(5)(G)

13. B: The Trail of Tears was the forcible removal of Native American tribes from their homes in the Southeastern US to Oklahoma. The name came due to the high number of Native Americans who died on the journey.

TEKS Standard §113.20(b)(7) and (8)

14. B: The Mason-Dixon Line, while established before the Civil War, was an effective line of demarcation between North and South during the Civil War. The line was originally a manifestation of a border dispute between Great Britain and the colonists.

TEKS Standard §113.20(b)(1) and (2)

15. B: New Amsterdam is now what we call New York City. It was called New Amsterdam by the majority Dutch settlers who initially colonized the area.

TEKS Standard §113.20(b)(1) and (2)

16. B: No evidence remains about the Roanoke Colony except that it did exist. Causes for its demise remain unknown.

- 49 -

TEKS Standard §113.20(b)(1)(A) and (6)

17. C: Meriwether Lewis and William Clark were the first to explore the Pacific Northwest region and Pacific coast beginning in 1806.

TEKS Standard §113.20(b)(7) and (11)(A) and (12)(A) and (12)(B)

18. C: Tobacco and cotton were the cash crops produced in the South. These were considered raw materials that could be shipped to the more industrial states to make finished products such as textiles and tobacco for smoking. The mild climate and moderate rainfall made this region ideal for growing these crops, in particular.

TEKS Standard §113.20(b)(12)(B)

19. C: The Triangle Slave Trade had the following stops: west coast of Africa for slaves, the West Indies for sugar or molasses and New England for manufacturing rum. These "commodities" were traded across nations and the triangle is a primary reason why prohibition and abolition were initially linked.

TEKS Standard §113.20(b)(15)

20. D: Americans pay federal income tax and elect officials to represent their interests in Congress and the Executive Branch of government. Taxes Americans pay is in proportion to their income and utilized to promote the interests of both majority and minority opinions.

TEKS Standard §113.20(b)(19)

21. B: A Writ of Habeas Corpus manifests in the accused person on trial in a court of law has the right to, and must be present to, defend himself for the trial to be held. The ideological roots of Habeas Corpus are in the Magna Carta.

TEKS Standard §113.20(b)(8)(b)

22. B: The Emancipation Proclamation (1863) effectively outlawed slavery in Northern States and made slavery illegal in states which were part of the Union. Southern states used this as fuel in their secession, in that they could not be in the Union and maintain slavery. The Union used the rebels' defiance to push southward in the battle theater during the Civil War.

TEKS Standard §113.20(b)(13)

23. B: Technological innovations such as interchangeable parts and the invention of the cotton gin catalyzed the industrial revolution in the second half of the 19th century. The pitfalls of child labor and unjust working conditions were part of the industrial revolution, but did not cause it. Immigration helped fuel the industrial revolution by providing a workforce.

TEKS Standard §113.20(b)(3)

24. B: The House of Commons is similar to the House of Representatives in that officials are elected by individuals to represent their interest in passing legislation.

TEKS Standard §113.20(b)(8)

25. B: Rebel states favored slavery, wore grey uniforms, favored states rights trumping federal law when the laws conflicted, and were the southern most states.

- 50 -

26. B: Lincoln's Gettysburg Address (1863) inspired and reminded Union forces that the Union was founded on individual liberty, and the rebels were violating the most critical principle the Founding Fathers sought to protect.

TEKS Standard §113.20(b)(21)

27. B: Members of the House of Representatives from each state are proportionate in number to the state's population. Therefore, the House is the purest form of representative government in our federal system.

TEKS Standard §113.20(b)(15)(A) and (17)(A)

28. C: Alexander Hamilton authored the Federalist Papers, which favored federal supremacy over state laws and the importance of a strong federal branch of government leadership.

TEKS Standard §113.20(b)(18)(B)

29. B: In the case of McCullough vs. Maryland (1819) a majority ruled on the side of the federal government on the unconstitutionality of a state tax on non-state currency. This decision set the precedent for a centrally produced and regulated currency, which the US now has as the Federal Reserve.

TEKS Standard §113.20(b)(4)

30. C: French rebels executed the King and Queen of France. American rebels did stage a violent rebellion, but did not execute any of the British Monarchy or civilian Brits.

TEKS Standard §113.20(b)(26)

31. D: The Planter's Northern Bride was the most famous work of "Anti-Tom" literature following the publication of Uncle Tom's Cabin. The African-American Experience is a fictitious title, but suggests some objectivity or respect for black citizens of the US The Narrative Life of Frederick Douglas is the work of Douglas regarding the progress he led towards civil rights, beginning in 1845, before the Civil War.

TEKS Standard §113.20(b)(7)

32. C: The Underground Railroad was not necessary literally a railroad, but a series of clandestine paths to move runaway and freed slaves out of Southern States prior to 1865.

TEKS Standard §113.20(b)(8)(C)

33. B: Lincoln stressed abolition as the focus in the Gettysburg Address.

TEKS Standard §113.20(b)(7) and (9)

34. B: Abolition, Prohibition, and Suffrage are linked via the Triangular Slave Trade and the reformation movements being led or supported by women.

TEKS Standard §113.20(b)(15)

35. A: The ideas and principals in John Locke's works from the late 17th century are reflected in the Bill of Rights: separation of church and state, free speech, and individual sovereignty.

TEKS Standard §113.20(b)(25)(A)

36. C: Deism posits that a Supernatural force created the world and universe, but that He did not intervene after creation. Jefferson wanted minimal central governing, as he viewed the Creator's relationship was with the universe.

TEKS Standard §113.20(b)(21)(B)

37. B: While abhorrent, a pamphlet written and distributed by a racist organization is permitted by the first amendment, the right to free speech.

TEKS Standard §113.20(b)(14)

38. A: Puritans valued self-sufficiency, hard work that would be rewarded by God in the after-life and on earth through success and in one's profession and family. Sins or laziness would be punished by lack of prosperity. The concept of survival of the fittest is congruent with capitalism: the best commodity will produce the most revenue, and inefficient production will cease. Free market capitalism, while secular, rewards performance.

TEKS Standard §113.20(b)(15)(D)

39. B: The President may veto legislation passed by Congress. The executive branch has this "check" on the legislative branch.

TEKS Standard §113.20(b)(3)

40. C: George Washington served 2 four-year terms as President. This interval of time was not specified in the Constitution, but future Presidents followed suit (until FDR).

TEKS Standard §113.20(b)(5)(E)

41. B: George Washington warned against potential pit-falls he foresaw in the future of the US: political factions, foreign allegiances that might compromise the sovereignty of the US, and too much state control, among others. Future presidents adopted his warning against foreign allegiances and kept the US largely out of international conflict until World War I.

TEKS Standard §113.20(b)(29)(C) and (29)(H)

42. C: The bison population was 30 million in 1800 and 200,000 in 1994.

TEKS Standard §113.20(b)(11)(B) and (29)(B)

43. D: Westward colonization via railroad lines facilitated bison hunting as a sport of frivolous loss. The bison population that existed before Americans moved westward was decimated, and has just in the past 20 years begun to replenish itself via conservation efforts by the Federal Government.

TEKS Standard §113.20(b)(29)(C) and (29)(H)

44. A: Baltimore is listed on the map as the 6th largest city.

TEKS Standard §113.20(b)(29)(C)

45. D: Western European countries were equally represented in the colonies, as is illustrated on the map.

TEKS Standard §113.20(b)(29)(C)

46. D: Colonies were settled in ports along the length of the eastern seaboard.

TEKS Standard §113.20(b)(29)(C)

47. D: England established Plymouth in 1620.

TEKS Standard §113.20(b)(29)(C)

48. D: Colonists established the first permanent settlement in North America during the 17th century.

Social Studies Practice Test #2

1. The three branches of government in the United States are called:

    a. Executive, legislative, and judicial
    b. Federal, state, and local
    c. National, constitutional, and representative
    d. Presidential, congressional, and legal

2. The three branches of federal government were enumerated in:

    a. The *Declaration of Independence*
    b. The first amendment
    c. The second amendment
    d. The *Constitution*

3. The first amendment is the first item in:

    a. The *Bill of Rights*
    b. The *Declaration of Independence*
    c. The *Emancipation Proclamation*
    d. The Writ *of Habeas Corpus*

4. The *Townshend Acts* of 1767 passed by British Parliament were:

    a. An attempt to provide representation of the colonies in Parliament
    b. An attempt to raise revenue following the Seven Years War
    c. An attempt to appease the demands of the Boston Tea Party
    d. An attempt to abide by the *Declaration of Independence*

5. The Seven Years War, called the French and Indian War by the Colonists:

    a. Was the precursor to the American Revolution
    b. Was a conflict related to European colonization
    c. Primarily took place in Canada
    d. Ended European conquests

6. Rum exported from _____ was made from sugar exported from the West Indies as a commodity in the West Indies slave triangle.

    a. Jamaica
    b. New England
    c. Southern France
    d. Western colonies

7. The *Magna Carta* influenced which of the following?

    a. Abolition
    b. The *Bill of Rights*
    c. Women's Suffrage
    d. The *Gettysburg Address*

8. Puritans fled Europe in order to:

    a. Become acquainted with potential native peoples

    b. Exercise freedom of the press

    c. Practice freedom of religion

    d. Reestablish the Holy Roman Empire

9. What type of leadership does the U.S. utilize?

    a. Monarchy

    b. Oligarchy

    c. Theocratic

    d. Republic

10. Cherokee people were forced out of the South during the mid-1800s. The forced evacuation is known as:

    a. The Appalachian Trail

    b. The Oregon Trail

    c. The Trail of Tears

    d. The Trail of No Return

11. What group of American colonists was led by William Penn, practiced pacifism, is also known as the Society of Friends, and believed in total equality among men?

    a. The Amish

    b. The Puritans

    c. The Quakers

    d. The Reformers

12. Guaranteed rights enumerated in the *Declaration of Independence*, possessed by all people, are referred to as:

    a. Universal rights

    b. Unalienable rights

    c. Voting rights

    d. Peoples' rights

13. Before the Civil War, to which of the following did Southern states object?

    a. An increase in Southern tobacco production

    b. An increase in tariffs on Northern manufactured goods

    c. An increase in western mining for gold

    d. An increase in the voting rights of slaves

14. The Mason-Dixon Line divided:

    a. The East from the West before the western states were incorporated

    b. The East from the West along the Mississippi River

    c. The North from the South before the Civil War

    d. The Senate from the House of Representatives

15. The 13 colonies did not include:

    a. Delaware
    b. Maine
    c. South Carolina
    d. Virginia

16. The American colony that left little evidence for historians was:

    a. New Amsterdam
    b. Norfolk
    c. Roanoke
    d. Williamsburg

17. The first successful English colony in the Americas was named for the English monarch who ruled during the early 1600s. A group of 104 English colonists settled in the Chesapeake Bay of modern-day Virginia, and initially befriended the Algonquin Indians. This colony was called:

    a. New South Wales
    b. New London
    c. Jamestown
    d. Georgeville

18. The Pacific Northwest was extensively explored by:

    a. Mason and Dixon
    b. Laurel and Hardy
    c. Lewis and Clark
    d. Washington and Jefferson

19. The mild climate and vast open spaces in the southern colonies were ideal for:

    a. Large, industrial factories
    b. Farming of a variety of cash crops
    c. Growing flowers and making pottery
    d. Railroad tracks and scenic tours

20. The Boston Tea Party was a protest against:

    a. Being able to grow American tea
    b. Being forced to drink tea in the Americas
    c. Being taxed by England without being represented in Parliament
    d. Being able to clean pollution out of Boston Harbor

21. The invention of interchangeable parts facilitated which of the following?

    a. The American Revolution
    b. The Feminist Revolution
    c. The French Revolution
    d. The Industrial Revolution

22. Southern plantation owners benefitted economically from which of the following?

    a. Freeing of slaves with the 13th amendment
    b. The invention of the cotton gin
    c. The American Revolution
    d. The invention of the automatic rifle

23. The Northern U.S. experienced economic growth during the 1800s largely as a result of:

    a. A new and continually growing railroad system
    b. The invention of the cotton gin
    c. Slavery
    d. Taxation

24. Freedom of speech is a right guaranteed by the *Constitution* in the *Bill of Rights*. What did early American colonists want to "speak freely" about, in particular?

    a. The King's Court
    b. The President
    c. Religious beliefs
    d. Slavery

25. Which entity in American government is the closest to true democracy?

    a. The Electoral College
    b. The House of Representatives
    c. Committees within the Senate
    d. The Supreme Court

26. Which box contains all the features of the Union during the Civil War?

a.	Abolition Blue Uniforms Federal Governance Southern States	c.	Abolition Blue Uniforms Federal Governance Northern States
b.	No Stance on Slavery Grey Uniforms States Rights Northern States	d.	No Stance on Slavery Grey Uniforms States Rights Southern States

27. Alexander Hamilton's legacy is reflected in what quality of American government?

    a. Democracy
    b. Federalism
    c. Loose constructionism
    d. States rights

28. *Marbury vs. Madison* was a landmark Supreme Court decision that established the precedent of judicial review. Judicial review is congruous with which of the following aspects of U.S. government?

    a. Checks and balances
    b. Federalism
    c. Separation of church and state
    d. States rights

29. Thomas Paine was considered a propagandist prior to the American Revolution. Which of these is one of his famous works that influenced American political ideology?

    a. *Common Sense*
    b. The *Declaration of Independence*
    c. The Writ *of Habeas Corpus*
    d. The *US Constitution*

30. The illustration below is taken from a novel entitled *The Planter's Northern Bride*, a reactionary novel directed against Harriet Beecher Stowe's novel, *Uncle Tom's Cabin*. *The Planter's Northern Bride* is a novel categorized in the genre known as "Anti-Tom literature." The perspective of the novel is likely:

    a. Abolitionist
    b. Pro-slavery
    c. Romantic
    d. Baroque

31. After the Civil War, urban populations increased. This growth was likely due to:

    a. An increased reliance on agriculture
    b. The Industrial Revolution
    c. Prohibition
    d. Slavery persisting in some areas

32. The French Revolution took inspiration from the American Revolution. How do the revolutions differ?

    a. The central government established by the revolution
    b. The violent overthrow of a monarchy
    c. The style of battle
    d. The populist political ideals

33. John Locke was a philosopher who influenced whom?

    a. American businessmen during the industrial revolution
    b. The French Monarchy during the French Revolution
    c. The founding fathers of the U.S.
    d. Southern soldiers during the Civil War

34. Thomas Jefferson embraced a theological philosophy called deism, which promotes which of the following?

    a. Abolition
    b. Atheism
    c. Separation of church and state
    d. A theocratic central government

35. Which of the following is not protected under the principal of freedom of speech?

    a. Yelling "boo" during a Presidential address for laughs
    b. Yelling "fire" at a public gathering as a false alarm
    c. Yelling "vote for Lincoln" at a pro-slavery rally
    d. Not talking when taken into police custody

36. The economic structure of the U.S. is primarily a system of free market capitalism. From what group in American history is capitalism likely drawn?

    a. Colonial Puritans
    b. Native Americans
    c. States rights advocates
    d. Plantation owners

37. The Presidential veto of legislation passed by Congress illustrates which principal in American government?

    a. Checks and balances
    b. Federal regulation
    c. Freedom of speech
    d. Separation of church and state

38. George Washington's farewell address and the *Monroe Doctrine* have which of the following in common

    a. Abolition
    b. Isolationism
    c. Presidential term limits
    d. Women's suffrage

39. The Articles of Confederation differ from the U.S. Constitution in what aspect?

    a. Abolition of slavery
    b. Federal deference to states rights
    c. Judicial supremacy
    d. Recognition of the British Throne

40. Representative democracy was likely motivated by:

    a. An increase in population
    b. Aristocracy
    c. The Supreme Court
    d. States passing laws that violated federal laws

Questions 41 – 44 pertain to the following map:

Agricultural Regions, 1900

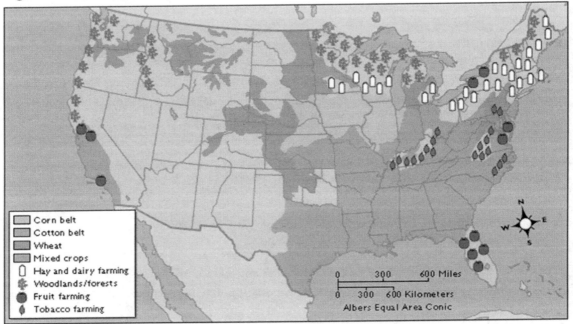

State	Inches of Rain per Year
California	17.28
Florida	49.91
New York	42.46

41. Which states were farming tobacco in 1900?

a. Florida, California, New York
b. Washington, Oregon, California
c. Kentucky, North Carolina, Virginia
d. Georgia, Alabama, Mississippi

42. Based on the map and the amount of rain per year, what can you extrapolate about fruit farming?

a. Oranges are grown in California, Florida, and New York
b. The amount of rain does not have an effect on fruit farming
c. California, Florida, and New York each grow different fruits
d. Nothing

43. What geographical feature related to average temperature do the woodland/forest areas share?

a. Approximately the same latitude
b. Approximately the same longitude
c. Mostly Eastern states
d. Mostly Western states

44. Approximately how wide, in miles, was the region of hay and dairy farming?
   a. 600 mi.
   b. 1,200 mi.
   c. 1,800 mi.
   d. 2,400 mi.

45. Passing of the *Homestead Act* resulting in the federal government giving out approximately 80 million acres of land from 1862 to 1900. What was the likely objective of the *Homestead Act*?
   a. To displace Native American peoples
   b. To encourage railroad construction
   c. To encourage western settlement and farming
   d. To create the Industrial Revolution

Questions 46 – 48 pertain to the following graph:

Union Membership, 1864–1921

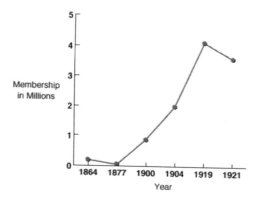

46. Labor union membership increased in conjunction with what other development in American history?
   a. The Gold Rush
   b. The Civil War
   c. The Industrial Revolution
   d. A decline in manufacturing

47. Approximately how many people were members of labor unions in 1900?
   a. 1
   b. 1 million
   c. 10 million
   d. 100 million

48. What is a possible explanation for the sharp decrease in membership around 1919?
   a. Abolition
   b. More laborers were being treated fairly
   c. Fewer people trusted labor unions
   d. Prohibition

- 61 -

Answer Key and Explanations for Social Studies Test #2

TEKS Standard §113.20(b)(3) and (15)(D)

1. A: The *Constitution* lists three branches of federal government. They are the executive branch, the legislative branch, and the judicial branch.

TEKS Standard §113.20(b)(15)(D)

2. D: The *Constitution* lists the three branches of federal government.

TEKS Standard §113.20(b)(19)(B)

3. A: The first amendment is the first item in the *Bill of Rights*.

TEKS Standard §113.20(b)(4)(A)

4. B: The Seven Years War (called the French and Indian War by colonists) was very costly for the British government. In order to raise revenue, the British levied taxes on colonists. The colonists resisted, largely because they had no representation in British Parliament.

TEKS Standard §113.20(b)(1)(A)

5. B: The Seven Years War was a global military conflict. In the Americas, the conflict was largely between Western European countries, Great Britain and France, in particular.

TEKS Standard §113.20(b)(12)(B)

6. B: The West Indies slave triangle's points are New England rum, West African slaves, and West Indies sugar or molasses.

TEKS Standard §113.20(b)(15)(A)

7. B: The *Magna Carta* is the first known mention of individual civil liberties as enumerated in the *Bill of Rights* of the *U.S. Constitution*.

TEKS Standard §113.20(b)(2)

8. C: Puritan colonists had been persecuted in Europe and sought religious freedom.

TEKS Standard §113.20(b)(3)

9. D: The U.S. is a republic: we elect representatives to vote on our behalf.

TEKS Standard §113.20(b)(5)(G)

10. C: The Trail of Tears was the forcible removal of Native American tribes from their homes in the Southeastern U.S. to Oklahoma. It was called such due to the high number of Native Americans who died on the journey.

TEKS Standard §113.20(b)(20)(A)

11. C: William Penn was a Quaker who settled what is now, Pennsylvania.

TEKS Standard §113.20(b)(19)(A)

12. B: "...endowed by their Creator with certain unalienable Rights," is excerpted from the Declaration of Independence. These rights are unable to be taken away from individuals, referring to the colonists' rights that Great Britain could not oppress.

TEKS Standard §113.20(b)(7)(A)

13. B: Southern states provided raw materials that were manufactured into commodities in Northern states. Southerners resented paying taxes to Northern states for these products (textiles, furniture, etc).

TEKS Standard §113.20(b)(7)

14. C: The Mason-Dixon Line was the manifestation of a border dispute between Great Britain and the colonists. It effectively separated, or illustrated a cultural divide between North and South before the Civil War.

TEKS Standard §113.20(b)(2) and (10)(A)

15. B: The 13 colonies were: Massachusetts, Rhode Island, Connecticut, New Hampshire, New York, Delaware, New Jersey, Pennsylvania, Virginia, Maryland, North Carolina, South Carolina and Georgia.

TEKS Standard §113.20(b)(10)(A)

16. C: There is no archeological or historical data of the Roanoke Colony, beyond that we know that there were colonists who settled there during the 17th century.

TEKS Standard §113.20(b)(1)(C) and (10)(A)

17. C: Jamestown was named for King James, and was the first colony of Great Britain to sustain itself.

TEKS Standard §113.20(b)(1)(A) and (6)

18. C: Meriwether Lewis and William Clark led the first expedition to the Pacific Northwest just after the turn of the 19th century.

TEKS Standard §113.20(b)(11)(A)

19. B: A temperate climate and moderate rainfall allowed for cotton and tobacco. Known as "cash crops," they were raw materials for manufactured goods such as textiles and tobacco smoking products, respectively.

TEKS Standard §113.20(b)(20)(C)

20. C: "Taxation without representation," is the infamous protest of colonists when they dumped tea into Boston Harbor. Great Britain levied many unjust taxes against the colonists, but the tax that "broke the camel's back," was the tax on black tea.

TEKS Standard §113.20(b)(27)(A)

21. D: The Industrial Revolution was catalyzed by assembly line production and interchangeable parts, e.g., those used to make the cotton gin and firearms invented by Eli Whitney. Manufacturing costs and time were drastically reduced with the advent of interchangeable parts.

TEKS Standard §113.20(b)(27)(A)

22. B: The cotton gin was particularly beneficial to Southern plantation owners because cotton was challenging to harvest and process manually. Cotton farmers could bring in a large crop to a local cotton gin to have it seeded and bailed.

TEKS Standard §113.20(b)(27)(D)

23. A: Railroads originating in the Northeast allowed manufactured goods to be exported to Southern states and Western territories.

TEKS Standard §113.20(b)(2)(B) and (3)(C) and (15)(D) and (25)

24. C: Religious persecution was an initial reason colonists fled to the Americas. By the time the *Bill of Rights* was written, the right to speak and write freely about government and religion were priority concerns.

TEKS Standard §113.20(b)(3)

25. B: Members of the House of Representatives are elected in proportion to the population of each state. Representation by senators is not based on population, and is therefore skewed in electoral weight. The Electoral College can and has contradicted the popular vote in the Presidential election.

TEKS Standard §113.20(b)(8)(B)

26. C: The Union was represented in blue military uniforms, was comprised of Northern states, generally supported abolition of slavery, and favored a central government that could trump laws passed by individual states.

TEKS Standard §113.20(b)(15)(A) and (17)(A)

27. B: Alexander Hamilton authored the *Federalist Papers* which later became the stance of the Union during the Civil War.

TEKS Standard §113.20(b)(18)(B)

28. A: The concept of checks and balances is manifested in the three branches of federal government and by the overlap of certain decisions by more than one branch. The President appoints the Supreme Court justices and reviews legislation passed by Congress. Judicial review is sometimes seen as the judiciary being activist or "legislating from the bench." However, the Supreme Court around the turn of the 19th century established the precedent that the Court could rule as unconstitutional, legislation it viewed was incongruous with the Constitution.

TEKS Standard §113.20(b)(4)(B)

29. A: Thomas Paine authored *Common Sense*, which argued for individual rights and against British oppression.

TEKS Standard §113.20(b)(26)

30. B: *Uncle Tom's Cabin* is the most famous abolitionist work of literature. There was some reactionary literature published after *UTC*, which presented arguments to preserve slavery, as it was not as horrific a picture as was painted by Northern intellectuals and non-slave owners. The illustration shows a white couple looking fondly at a kneeling black man, presumably slave. While the black man is in a subservient position, kneeling, he does not look like he has been mistreated.

TEKS Standard §113.20(b)(27)(B)

31. B: Growth of industry was concentrated in urban areas, which cyclically drew laborers into cities, growing the population of cities and increasing efficiency and quality in industry.

TEKS Standard §113.20(b)(4)

32. B: French rebels executed the King and Queen of France. American rebels did stage a violent rebellion, but did not execute any of the British monarchy or civilian Brits.

TEKS Standard §113.20(b)(20)(A)

33. C: John Locke was a 17th century philosopher who introduced many of the concepts embraced by the Enlightenment such as individual worth, knowledge gained by experience and empirical evidence. He also advocated for religious tolerance, separation of church and state, and the illegitimacy of monarchy.

TEKS Standard §113.20(b)(4)(B)

34. C: Thomas Jefferson embraced John Locke's concept of separation of church and state. Deism posits that a Supernatural force created the world and universe, but that He did not intervene after creation. Jefferson wanted minimal central governing, just as he viewed the Creator's relationship with the universe.

TEKS Standard §113.20(b)(19)

35. B: Freedom of speech, as mentioned in the *Bill of Rights*, does not include speech that is deceptive and causes others harm, e.g. yelling "fire!" when there is no fire in a crowded theatre.

TEKS Standard §113.20(b)(14)

36. A: Puritans valued self-sufficiency and hard work that would be rewarded by God in the after-life and on earth by success in one's profession and family. Sins or laziness would be punished by a lack of prosperity. The concept of survival of the fittest is congruent with capitalism: the best commodity will produce the most revenue, and inefficient production will be replaced.

TEKS Standard §113.20(b)(15)(D)

37. A: Presidents may veto legislation passed by both houses of Congress, and in turn, Congress can override a Presidential veto with a 2/3 majority. These governmental practices are a further manifestation that each branch of government is watched by the other branches and, when necessary, can undo a decision it deems ill-advised or unconstitutional.

TEKS Standard §113.20(b)(5)(E)

38. B: George Washington warned against potential pit-falls he foresaw in the future of the U.S.: political factions, foreign allegiances that might compromise U.S. sovereignty of the, and too much state control, among others. Future Presidents adopted his warning against foreign allegiances which kept the U.S. largely out of international conflict until World War I.

TEKS Standard §113.20(b)(15)(B) and (15)(D)

39. B: The *Articles of Confederation* were the first attempt at a U.S. constitution. The *Articles* empowered the states much more than a central government. States rights would trump federal law under the *Articles*. This relationship was changed, of course, in the *Constitution*.

TEKS Standard §113.20(b)(3)

40. A: Representative government, by which citizens elect officials who share their views and who, in turn, present their views in a democratic system, is not a true democracy in which each individual votes on each issue. As the population of a democracy grows, the practicality of every individual voting on every issue becomes prohibitive to the process.

TEKS Standard §113.20(b)(29)(C) and (29)(J)

41. C: The map illustrates tobacco farming by the diamond-leaf shaped symbols in Kentucky, North Carolina, and Virginia.

TEKS Standard §113.20(b)(29)(C) and (29)(J)

42. C: Fruits are illustrated as being grown in California, New York, and Florida.

TEKS Standard §113.20(b)(29)(C) and (29)(J)

43. A: Woodlands and Forests are shown in the Pacific Northwest, North Central States, and Northeastern states. These states share the same range of latitudes as indicated on the map (as opposed to topography, rainfall, or some other influence on flora).

TEKS Standard §113.20(b)(29)(C) and (29)(H) and (29)(J)

44. C: Using the miles scale on the map, the hay and dairy region is approximately 1800 miles across.

TEKS Standard §113.20(b)(9)(D)

45. C: Passage of the *Homestead Act* encouraged people to move west by offering free or cheap land grants and/or money to begin a farm.

TEKS Standard §113.20(b)(29)(C) and (29)(D)

46. C: Labor unions began to form after the beginning of the Industrial Revolution as laborers began to suffer under the economic control of company owners. Laborers began to organize for individual rights in manufacturing settings such as safety, working hours, age of laborers, and wages. Agricultural enterprises did not have the same density of workers or potential for dangerous work environments.

- 66 -

TEKS Standard §113.20(b)(29)(C) and (29)(H)

47. B: The y-axis of the graph shows approximately 1 million on the x-axis of 1900.

TEKS Standard §113.20(b)(29)(C) and (29)(D)

48. D: Prohibition during the 1920's coincided with the drop in labor union membership. Illegitimate manufacturing of alcohol and organized crime were counter to the formation of labor unions.

- 67 -

How to Overcome Test Anxiety

Just the thought of taking a test is enough to make most people a little nervous. A test is an important event that can have a long-term impact on your future, so it's important to take it seriously and it's natural to feel anxious about performing well. But just because anxiety is normal, that doesn't mean that it's helpful in test taking, or that you should simply accept it as part of your life. Anxiety can have a variety of effects. These effects can be mild, like making you feel slightly nervous, or severe, like blocking your ability to focus or remember even a simple detail.

If you experience test anxiety—whether severe or mild—it's important to know how to beat it. To discover this, first you need to understand what causes test anxiety.

Causes of Test Anxiety

While we often think of anxiety as an uncontrollable emotional state, it can actually be caused by simple, practical things. One of the most common causes of test anxiety is that a person does not feel adequately prepared for their test. This feeling can be the result of many different issues such as poor study habits or lack of organization, but the most common culprit is time management. Starting to study too late, failing to organize your study time to cover all of the material, or being distracted while you study will mean that you're not well prepared for the test. This may lead to cramming the night before, which will cause you to be physically and mentally exhausted for the test. Poor time management also contributes to feelings of stress, fear, and hopelessness as you realize you are not well prepared but don't know what to do about it.

Other times, test anxiety is not related to your preparation for the test but comes from unresolved fear. This may be a past failure on a test, or poor performance on tests in general. It may come from comparing yourself to others who seem to be performing better or from the stress of living up to expectations. Anxiety may be driven by fears of the future—how failure on this test would affect your educational and career goals. These fears are often completely irrational, but they can still negatively impact your test performance.

> **Review Video: 3 Reasons You Have Test Anxiety**
> Visit mometrix.com/academy and enter code: 428468

Elements of Test Anxiety

As mentioned earlier, test anxiety is considered to be an emotional state, but it has physical and mental components as well. Sometimes you may not even realize that you are suffering from test anxiety until you notice the physical symptoms. These can include trembling hands, rapid heartbeat, sweating, nausea, and tense muscles. Extreme anxiety may lead to fainting or vomiting. Obviously, any of these symptoms can have a negative impact on testing. It is important to recognize them as soon as they begin to occur so that you can address the problem before it damages your performance.

> **Review Video:** <u>3 Ways to Tell You Have Test Anxiety</u>
> Visit mometrix.com/academy and enter code: 927847

The mental components of test anxiety include trouble focusing and inability to remember learned information. During a test, your mind is on high alert, which can help you recall information and stay focused for an extended period of time. However, anxiety interferes with your mind's natural processes, causing you to blank out, even on the questions you know well. The strain of testing during anxiety makes it difficult to stay focused, especially on a test that may take several hours. Extreme anxiety can take a huge mental toll, making it difficult not only to recall test information but even to understand the test questions or pull your thoughts together.

> **Review Video:** <u>How Test Anxiety Affects Memory</u>
> Visit mometrix.com/academy and enter code: 609003

Effects of Test Anxiety

Test anxiety is like a disease—if left untreated, it will get progressively worse. Anxiety leads to poor performance, and this reinforces the feelings of fear and failure, which in turn lead to poor performances on subsequent tests. It can grow from a mild nervousness to a crippling condition. If allowed to progress, test anxiety can have a big impact on your schooling, and consequently on your future.

Test anxiety can spread to other parts of your life. Anxiety on tests can become anxiety in any stressful situation, and blanking on a test can turn into panicking in a job situation. But fortunately, you don't have to let anxiety rule your testing and determine your grades. There are a number of relatively simple steps you can take to move past anxiety and function normally on a test and in the rest of life.

> **Review Video:** <u>How Test Anxiety Impacts Your Grades</u>
> Visit mometrix.com/academy and enter code: 939819

Physical Steps for Beating Test Anxiety

While test anxiety is a serious problem, the good news is that it can be overcome. It doesn't have to control your ability to think and remember information. While it may take time, you can begin taking steps today to beat anxiety.

Just as your first hint that you may be struggling with anxiety comes from the physical symptoms, the first step to treating it is also physical. Rest is crucial for having a clear, strong mind. If you are tired, it is much easier to give in to anxiety. But if you establish good sleep habits, your body and mind will be ready to perform optimally, without the strain of exhaustion. Additionally, sleeping well helps you to retain information better, so you're more likely to recall the answers when you see the test questions.

Getting good sleep means more than going to bed on time. It's important to allow your brain time to relax. Take study breaks from time to time so it doesn't get overworked, and don't study right before bed. Take time to rest your mind before trying to rest your body, or you may find it difficult to fall asleep.

> **Review Video: The Importance of Sleep for Your Brain**
> Visit mometrix.com/academy and enter code: 319338

Along with sleep, other aspects of physical health are important in preparing for a test. Good nutrition is vital for good brain function. Sugary foods and drinks may give a burst of energy but this burst is followed by a crash, both physically and emotionally. Instead, fuel your body with protein and vitamin-rich foods.

Also, drink plenty of water. Dehydration can lead to headaches and exhaustion, especially if your brain is already under stress from the rigors of the test. Particularly if your test is a long one, drink water during the breaks. And if possible, take an energy-boosting snack to eat between sections.

> **Review Video: How Diet Can Affect your Mood**
> Visit mometrix.com/academy and enter code: 624317

Along with sleep and diet, a third important part of physical health is exercise. Maintaining a steady workout schedule is helpful, but even taking 5-minute study breaks to walk can help get your blood pumping faster and clear your head. Exercise also releases endorphins, which contribute to a positive feeling and can help combat test anxiety.

When you nurture your physical health, you are also contributing to your mental health. If your body is healthy, your mind is much more likely to be healthy as well. So take time to rest, nourish your body with healthy food and water, and get moving as much as possible. Taking these physical steps will make you stronger and more able to take the mental steps necessary to overcome test anxiety.

> **Review Video: How to Stay Healthy and Prevent Test Anxiety**
> Visit mometrix.com/academy and enter code: 877894

Mental Steps for Beating Test Anxiety

Working on the mental side of test anxiety can be more challenging, but as with the physical side, there are clear steps you can take to overcome it. As mentioned earlier, test anxiety often stems from lack of preparation, so the obvious solution is to prepare for the test. Effective studying may be the most important weapon you have for beating test anxiety, but you can and should employ several other mental tools to combat fear.

First, boost your confidence by reminding yourself of past success—tests or projects that you aced. If you're putting as much effort into preparing for this test as you did for those, there's no reason you should expect to fail here. Work hard to prepare; then trust your preparation.

Second, surround yourself with encouraging people. It can be helpful to find a study group, but be sure that the people you're around will encourage a positive attitude. If you spend time with others who are anxious or cynical, this will only contribute to your own anxiety. Look for others who are motivated to study hard from a desire to succeed, not from a fear of failure.

Third, reward yourself. A test is physically and mentally tiring, even without anxiety, and it can be helpful to have something to look forward to. Plan an activity following the test, regardless of the outcome, such as going to a movie or getting ice cream.

When you are taking the test, if you find yourself beginning to feel anxious, remind yourself that you know the material. Visualize successfully completing the test. Then take a few deep, relaxing breaths and return to it. Work through the questions carefully but with confidence, knowing that you are capable of succeeding.

Developing a healthy mental approach to test taking will also aid in other areas of life. Test anxiety affects more than just the actual test—it can be damaging to your mental health and even contribute to depression. It's important to beat test anxiety before it becomes a problem for more than testing.

> **Review Video: Test Anxiety and Depression**
> Visit mometrix.com/academy and enter code: 904704

Study Strategy

Being prepared for the test is necessary to combat anxiety, but what does being prepared look like? You may study for hours on end and still not feel prepared. What you need is a strategy for test prep. The next few pages outline our recommended steps to help you plan out and conquer the challenge of preparation.

Step 1: Scope Out the Test

Learn everything you can about the format (multiple choice, essay, etc.) and what will be on the test. Gather any study materials, course outlines, or sample exams that may be available. Not only will this help you to prepare, but knowing what to expect can help to alleviate test anxiety.

Step 2: Map Out the Material

Look through the textbook or study guide and make note of how many chapters or sections it has. Then divide these over the time you have. For example, if a book has 15 chapters and you have five days to study, you need to cover three chapters each day. Even better, if you have the time, leave an extra day at the end for overall review after you have gone through the material in depth.

If time is limited, you may need to prioritize the material. Look through it and make note of which sections you think you already have a good grasp on, and which need review. While you are studying, skim quickly through the familiar sections and take more time on the challenging parts. Write out your plan so you don't get lost as you go. Having a written plan also helps you feel more in control of the study, so anxiety is less likely to arise from feeling overwhelmed at the amount to cover. A sample plan may look like this:

- Day 1: Skim chapters 1–4, study chapter 5 (especially pages 31–33)
- Day 2: Study chapters 6–7, skim chapters 8–9
- Day 3: Skim chapter 10, study chapters 11–12 (especially pages 87–90)
- Day 4: Study chapters 13–15
- Day 5: Overall review (focus most on chapters 5, 6, and 12), take practice test

Step 3: Gather Your Tools

Decide what study method works best for you. Do you prefer to highlight in the book as you study and then go back over the highlighted portions? Or do you type out notes of the important information? Or is it helpful to make flashcards that you can carry with you? Assemble the pens, index cards, highlighters, post-it notes, and any other materials you may need so you won't be distracted by getting up to find things while you study.

If you're having a hard time retaining the information or organizing your notes, experiment with different methods. For example, try color-coding by subject with colored pens, highlighters, or post-it notes. If you learn better by hearing, try recording yourself reading your notes so you can listen while in the car, working out, or simply sitting at your desk. Ask a friend to quiz you from your flashcards, or try teaching someone the material to solidify it in your mind.

Step 4: Create Your Environment

It's important to avoid distractions while you study. This includes both the obvious distractions like visitors and the subtle distractions like an uncomfortable chair (or a too-comfortable couch that makes you want to fall asleep). Set up the best study environment possible: good lighting and a comfortable work area. If background music helps you focus, you may want to turn it on, but otherwise keep the room quiet. If you are using a computer to take notes, be sure you don't have any other windows open, especially applications like social media, games, or anything else that could distract you. Silence your phone and turn off notifications. Be sure to keep water close by so you stay hydrated while you study (but avoid unhealthy drinks and snacks).

Also, take into account the best time of day to study. Are you freshest first thing in the morning? Try to set aside some time then to work through the material. Is your mind clearer in the afternoon or evening? Schedule your study session then. Another method is to study at the same time of day that you will take the test, so that your brain gets used to working on the material at that time and will be ready to focus at test time.

Step 5: Study!

Once you have done all the study preparation, it's time to settle into the actual studying. Sit down, take a few moments to settle your mind so you can focus, and begin to follow your study plan. Don't give in to distractions or let yourself procrastinate. This is your time to prepare so you'll be ready to fearlessly approach the test. Make the most of the time and stay focused.

Of course, you don't want to burn out. If you study too long you may find that you're not retaining the information very well. Take regular study breaks. For example, taking five minutes out of every hour to walk briskly, breathing deeply and swinging your arms, can help your mind stay fresh.

As you get to the end of each chapter or section, it's a good idea to do a quick review. Remind yourself of what you learned and work on any difficult parts. When you feel that you've mastered the material, move on to the next part. At the end of your study session, briefly skim through your notes again.

But while review is helpful, cramming last minute is NOT. If at all possible, work ahead so that you won't need to fit all your study into the last day. Cramming overloads your brain with more information than it can process and retain, and your tired mind may struggle to recall even previously learned information when it is overwhelmed with last-minute study. Also, the urgent nature of cramming and the stress placed on your brain contribute to anxiety. You'll be more likely to go to the test feeling unprepared and having trouble thinking clearly.

So don't cram, and don't stay up late before the test, even just to review your notes at a leisurely pace. Your brain needs rest more than it needs to go over the information again. In fact, plan to finish your studies by noon or early afternoon the day before the test. Give your brain the rest of the day to relax or focus on other things, and get a good night's sleep. Then you will be fresh for the test and better able to recall what you've studied.

Step 6: Take a practice test

Many courses offer sample tests, either online or in the study materials. This is an excellent resource to check whether you have mastered the material, as well as to prepare for the test format and environment.

Check the test format ahead of time: the number of questions, the type (multiple choice, free response, etc.), and the time limit. Then create a plan for working through them. For example, if you have 30 minutes to take a 60-question test, your limit is 30 seconds per question. Spend less time on the questions you know well so that you can take more time on the difficult ones.

If you have time to take several practice tests, take the first one open book, with no time limit. Work through the questions at your own pace and make sure you fully understand them. Gradually work up to taking a test under test conditions: sit at a desk with all study materials put away and set a timer. Pace yourself to make sure you finish the test with time to spare and go back to check your answers if you have time.

After each test, check your answers. On the questions you missed, be sure you understand why you missed them. Did you misread the question (tests can use tricky wording)? Did you forget the information? Or was it something you hadn't learned? Go back and study any shaky areas that the practice tests reveal.

Taking these tests not only helps with your grade, but also aids in combating test anxiety. If you're already used to the test conditions, you're less likely to worry about it, and working through tests until you're scoring well gives you a confidence boost. Go through the practice tests until you feel comfortable, and then you can go into the test knowing that you're ready for it.

Test Tips

On test day, you should be confident, knowing that you've prepared well and are ready to answer the questions. But aside from preparation, there are several test day strategies you can employ to maximize your performance.

First, as stated before, get a good night's sleep the night before the test (and for several nights before that, if possible). Go into the test with a fresh, alert mind rather than staying up late to study.

Try not to change too much about your normal routine on the day of the test. It's important to eat a nutritious breakfast, but if you normally don't eat breakfast at all, consider eating just a protein bar. If you're a coffee drinker, go ahead and have your normal coffee. Just make sure you time it so that the caffeine doesn't wear off right in the middle of your test. Avoid sugary beverages, and drink enough water to stay hydrated but not so much that you need a restroom break 10 minutes into the test. If your test isn't first thing in the morning, consider going for a walk or doing a light workout before the test to get your blood flowing.

Allow yourself enough time to get ready, and leave for the test with plenty of time to spare so you won't have the anxiety of scrambling to arrive in time. Another reason to be early is to select a good seat. It's helpful to sit away from doors and windows, which can be distracting. Find a good seat, get out your supplies, and settle your mind before the test begins.

When the test begins, start by going over the instructions carefully, even if you already know what to expect. Make sure you avoid any careless mistakes by following the directions.

Then begin working through the questions, pacing yourself as you've practiced. If you're not sure on an answer, don't spend too much time on it, and don't let it shake your confidence. Either skip it and come back later, or eliminate as many wrong answers as possible and guess among the remaining ones. Don't dwell on these questions as you continue—put them out of your mind and focus on what lies ahead.

Be sure to read all of the answer choices, even if you're sure the first one is the right answer. Sometimes you'll find a better one if you keep reading. But don't second-guess yourself if you do immediately know the answer. Your gut instinct is usually right. Don't let test anxiety rob you of the information you know.

If you have time at the end of the test (and if the test format allows), go back and review your answers. Be cautious about changing any, since your first instinct tends to be correct, but make sure you didn't misread any of the questions or accidentally mark the wrong answer choice. Look over any you skipped and make an educated guess.

At the end, leave the test feeling confident. You've done your best, so don't waste time worrying about your performance or wishing you could change anything. Instead, celebrate the successful completion of this test. And finally, use this test to learn how to deal with anxiety even better next time.

> **Review Video:** <u>5 Tips to Beat Test Anxiety</u>
> Visit mometrix.com/academy and enter code: 570656

Important Qualification

Not all anxiety is created equal. If your test anxiety is causing major issues in your life beyond the classroom or testing center, or if you are experiencing troubling physical symptoms related to your anxiety, it may be a sign of a serious physiological or psychological condition. If this sounds like your situation, we strongly encourage you to seek professional help.

Thank You

We at Mometrix would like to extend our heartfelt thanks to you, our friend and patron, for allowing us to play a part in your journey. It is a privilege to serve people from all walks of life who are unified in their commitment to building the best future they can for themselves.

The preparation you devote to these important testing milestones may be the most valuable educational opportunity you have for making a real difference in your life. We encourage you to put your heart into it—that feeling of succeeding, overcoming, and yes, conquering will be well worth the hours you've invested.

We want to hear your story, your struggles and your successes, and if you see any opportunities for us to improve our materials so we can help others even more effectively in the future, please share that with us as well. **The team at Mometrix would be absolutely thrilled to hear from you!** So please, send us an email (support@mometrix.com) and let's stay in touch.

If you'd like some additional help, check out these other resources we offer for your exam:

http://MometrixFlashcards.com/STAAR

Additional Bonus Material

Due to our efforts to try to keep this book to a manageable length, we've created a link that will give you access to all of your additional bonus material.

Please visit https://www.mometrix.com/bonus948/staarg8socst to access the information.